100 Great Lite Bites

100 Great Lite Bites

high energy · fast food · naturally healthy

Silvana Franco

CASSELL ILLUSTRATED

First published in Great Britain in 2006 by Cassell Illustrated,
a division of Octopus Publishing Group Limited, 2-4 Heron Quays, London E14 4JP

Distributed in the United States of America by
Sterling Publishing Co., Inc., 387 Park Avenue South, New York, NY 10016-8810

A CIP catalog record for this book is available from the British Library.

ISBN-13: 978-1-844035-39-7
ISBN-10: 1-844035-39-5

10 9 8 7 6 5 4 3 2 1

Photography by Craig Robertson
Design by John Round
Editor Barbara Dixon
Art Director Auberon Hedgecoe
Publishing Manager Anna Cheifetz
Printed in China

Contents

Introduction

So, Great Lite Bites—natural, organic produce used to make delicious, recipes to fill any gap—big or small. This book is a selection of my most favorite everyday dishes. It's about making the way you cook and eat fit into the way you choose to live your life. Simple, tasty food that everyone can cook and enjoy and it just happens to be good for you too. Fruity porridge, freshly blended juices, wholesome soups, giant salads, and delicious desserts such as Buttermilk baked custard— you and your family will love these dishes and they will love you right back!

Be healthy

We are all used to hearing that "you are what you eat" and most of us accept that this is true. If you feed your body the best possible source of fuel, then it will thrive.

What you eat is the key to how you feel. Choose natural and wholesome, choose fruit and vegetables, brown before white and, where possible, unrefined. Add the odd treat once in a while, a fruity dessert, a square of dark chocolate, or the odd glass of wine if you want it, and you will find you are eating a healthy, balanced diet and feeling great. Most importantly of all, you will be choosing to eat food that you enjoy. Unrefined, natural food really does taste best.

Organic

I strongly recommend buying organic wherever possible. When it comes to fresh fruit and vegetables, it is especially important if you plan to eat the skin— as for baked potatoes, juicing, and ready-to-eat fresh fruit. All non-organic fresh fruit and vegetables must be peeled before use. There are many reasons why I fly the organic flag, but here are my top five:

1. Pesticides, herbicides, and a host of other chemicals routinely sprayed on conventionally grown fruit and vegetables can seriously damage your health.
2. Fresh organic produce on average contains one and a half times the vitamins, minerals, enzymes, and other nutrients of nonorganic goods.
3. Organic animals are not treated with antibiotics, hormones, and other medicines systematically used on intensively reared animals. Nor are they fed GM foods.
4. Organic produce, on the whole, tastes much better.
5. Organic food is now more widely available and the price difference is lowering all the time.

So, there's no excuse for skimping. Choose organic meat and free-range eggs and try subscribing to a regular fruit and vegetable box scheme. Most of the schemes operate in the same way by offering a range of different-size boxes containing a selection of seasonal produce. The produce normally goes from the supplier straight to the distributor, cutting out the store in between, so you may be surprised to find it's not as expensive as you might expect. Occasionally, you can find yourself with a surplus of something or other, but remember, if you can't juice it, you can almost certainly make a soup out of it! So, all that remains is to get down to the cooking...
Silvana

Breakfast on the go

Creamy ricotta omelet on toast

This recipe is by my pal, food writer Angela Boggiano, who has taken her inspiration from the Spanish classic tortilla. Her addition of ricotta and mint gives the omelet a fantastic flavor and texture. Perfect for a laid-back breakfast or lunch. You can also switch the mint for pancetta.

1 Preheat the broiler to medium. Drop the new potatoes into a small pan and cover with water. Bring to a boil and simmer for 15 minutes, or until tender. Drain and let cool slightly, then slice thinly.

2 Heat the oil in a large skillet with a heat-proof handle and cook the scallions for just a minute, then add the potatoes, peas, and fava beans to the pan.

3 Mix the mint into the beaten eggs along with some salt and pepper, then pour over the vegetables in the pan. Dollop tablespoons of ricotta on top and cook gently over medium heat until the base of the omelet is set and golden. Sprinkle the crumbled Parmesan on top.

4 Meanwhile toast the bread under the broiler and then place on serving plates.

5 Place the omelet under the broiler and cook until golden and just set. Slice into wedges and serve on the toasts sprinkled with salad cress and plenty of ground black pepper.

Serves 2

7 oz/200 g small new potatoes

1 tablespoon extra virgin olive oil

1 bunch scallions, chopped

½ cup frozen peas

½ cup fava beans

3 tablespoons chopped fresh mint

4 eggs, beaten

scant ½ cup ricotta cheese

small piece of Parmesan cheese, crumbled

4 slices crusty whole-grain bread or sourdough bread

4 oz/125 g pot salad cress

sea salt and freshly ground black pepper

Mapled brown bread clusters

These lovely little nutty clusters are wonderful with milk or yogurt.

Makes/serves 8

7 oz/200 g brown bread

generous ⅓ cup pecans, finely chopped

¼ teaspoon ground cinnamon

¾ stick butter, melted

4 tablespoons maple syrup

3 tablespoons light muscovado sugar

1 Preheat the oven to 325°F/160°C. Whiz the bread in a food processor to form rough crumbs. Tip into a bowl and stir in the nuts, cinnamon, butter, syrup, and sugar.

2 Spread out on a large cookie sheet and bake in the oven for 20–25 minutes, or until golden and crusty. Let cool, then break up any large clumps. Store in an airtight container.

Tea-steeped fruit salad

This takes a little bit of preparation the night before, but it will yield enough for breakfast for four days and, honestly, if you eat it for four consecutive days you will feel fantastic.

Serves 4

3 Earl Grey tea bags

3 cups boiling water

½ cup pitted prunes

scant ⅔ cup dried unsulfured apricots

scant ⅔ cup large raisins

½ cup dried cranberries or blueberries

grated rind and juice of 1 unwaxed orange

plain yogurt and chopped hazelnuts or almonds, to serve

1 Use the tea bags and boiling water to make tea and let stand for 10 minutes.

2 Place all the fruit in a pan, then pour in the tea (take out the bags) and bring back to a boil, then remove from the heat and let cool.

3 Stir in the orange rind and juice and chill for a few hours before eating.

4 To serve, spoon into bowls and top with the yogurt and nuts.

Potted Fruity Porridge

Such a brilliant summer breakfast! Make it the night before, forget about it, go to bed, and you'll be delighted when you get up and find it waiting in the refrigerator for you. If you're running late, just pop the pot into your bag and eat it when you get to work.

Makes 4 small pots

⅓ cup oatmeal

1½ cups whole milk

8 dried apricots, chopped

2 tablespoons small golden raisins

1–2 tablespoons light muscovado sugar

a pinch of salt

1 ripe peach, halved and pitted

1 Place the oatmeal, milk, apricots, golden raisins, sugar, and salt in a small pan and gently heat together for 10 minutes.

2 Chop the peach and stir into the porridge and simmer for an additional 5 minutes or so until the oats are tender and the mixture is thick and creamy.

3 Spoon into 4 small ramekins or pots and let cool, then cover and chill.

Honey Porridge

If you're making it just for you, eat one portion warm, then chill the other half and eat it cold the next day. Yum!

Serves 2

⅓ cup oatmeal

1 tablespoon wheat bran

generous ¾ cup water

¾ cup whole milk

1 tablespoon golden superfine sugar

a pinch of salt

2–4 tablespoons clear honey

1 Place the oatmeal, bran, water, milk, salt, and sugar in a small pan and gently heat together for 10–15 minutes, or until the oats are tender and the mixture is thick and creamy.

2 Spoon into 2 small bowls, then drizzle over the honey and serve.

Walnut bran muffins

Honestly, they taste lovely!

1 Preheat the oven to 375°F/190°C. Line a 12-hole muffin pan with paper cake cases.

2 Gently warm the buttermilk, just for a minute or 2, taking care not to let it boil. Place the cereal in a large heatproof bowl, then pour over the warm buttermilk and set aside for 5 minutes.

3 Mash the bananas and stir into the cereal along with the sugar, egg, and butter.

4 Gently fold in the flour and nuts, then spoon the mixture into the paper cake cases in the muffin tin. Push a date into the center of each muffin, then bake in the oven for 20–25 minutes, or until cooked through and nicely browned.

Makes 12

1¼ cups buttermilk

9 oz/250 g All-Bran cereal

2 ripe bananas

generous ½ cup light muscovado sugar

1 egg, beaten

1 stick butter, melted

2⅔ cups self-rising flour

1 cup chopped walnuts

12 dates

Spiced berry biscuits

Biscuits are sturdy enough to survive a journey in your pocket, so they make a great choice for breakfast on the run. These are flavorful enough to eat plain or toasted, but are even better split and sandwiched with soft cheese. And they freeze really well, too—make them over the weekend and cool, then pack two at a time into ziplock bags and freeze. Just remember to take a bag out of the freezer before you go to bed so they're ready for the morning!

1 Preheat the oven to 425°F/220°C. Place all the flour in a large bowl, then rub in the butter. Using a table knife, stir in the sugar, berries, allspice, and salt, then add the milk and stir in—if it feels a little dry, add a touch more milk, then bring together to make a soft dough.

2 Lightly dust the surface with a little flour, then roll out the dough no thinner than 1 inch/2.5 cm. Using a 2-inch/5-cm plain cutter, firmly stamp out the circles—try not to twist the cutter, as this makes the biscuits rise unevenly. Re-roll the trimmings and stamp out more circles.

3 Transfer the circles to a nonstick cookie sheet and dust with a little more flour, then bake in the oven for 12–15 minutes, or until well risen and golden. Cool on a cooling rack and serve just warm or at room temperature. They last only a day or two, so freeze any you don't eat.

Makes 12

scant ⅔ cup whole-wheat flour

1 cup self-rising flour, plus extra for dusting

½ stick butter, at room temperature

¼ cup golden superfine sugar

¾ cup dried mixed berries or cranberries

½ teaspoon ground allspice

a pinch of salt

⅔ cup whole milk

Pumpkin seed and apricot energy bars

Here is my version of those high-energy cereal bars you can buy. These are delicious, quite chewy, and full of goodness.

1 Stir the sugar into the condensed milk and set aside to dissolve.

2 Preheat the oven to 350°F/180°C. In a large bowl, mix the apricots with the oats, seeds, nuts, and cereal. Stir in the condensed milk until well blended.

3 Spoon the mixture into a nonstick 5 x 10-inch/12 x 25-cm pan, pressing down to ensure an even surface. Bake in the oven for 20–25 minutes, or until golden, then remove from the oven and let cool in the pan.

4 Turn out of the pan and cut into 16 bars. Wrap each one in a rectangle of waxed paper and store in an airtight container.

Makes 16

1 tablespoon dark muscovado sugar

1 cup whole condensed milk

generous 1 cup soft dried unsulfured apricots, coarsely chopped

1 cup oatmeal

generous ⅓ cup pumpkin seeds

⅓ cup whole almonds, coarsely chopped

1 cup puffed whole-grain rice cereal

Potato and scallion pancakes

What a weekend treat! Especially when topped with a few waves of smoked salmon, a soft-cooked egg, or a couple of crisp strips of lean bacon with the rind still on. There are so many interesting flours around now to experiment with. I love these pancakes made with buckwheat flour, but try with other types and see what hits the right note for you.

1 Boil the potatoes until tender, then mash thoroughly—lumps will really spoil the pancakes, so it is worth passing them through a ricer or a mouli grater.

2 Stir in the milk, flour, scallions, and salt to taste and let cool for 5 minutes. When the mash is cool enough not to set the eggs, stir in the yolks.

3 In a separate bowl, whisk the egg whites until softly peaking, then fold into the potato mixture.

4 Brush a nonstick skillet with a little oil and heat until hot. Drop spoonfuls of the batter into the hot pan and cook for a couple of minutes or so on each side until puffed and golden. Serve warm.

Makes 12 pancakes

1 lb 2 oz/500 g white potatoes, peeled and cubed

½ cup whole milk

⅓ cup self-rising flour

1 bunch of scallions, thinly sliced

3 eggs, separated

sea salt

olive oil, for frying

The morning-after cure

Yes, we know, "never again"! You feel shocking and think you want a can of cola, but no, actually this is what'll get you back on your feet again—and for more than five minutes. It's easy to drink and loaded with vitamins and some natural sugar for instant energy. Follow this with a Spiced berry biscuit (page 15) or some whole-grain toast, and you'll feel as good as new.

Serves 1

4 large carrots, cut into large chunks

2 red apples, cut into wedges

pulp and seeds from 2 passion fruit

Juice the carrots and apples, then stir in the passion fruit pulp and seeds. Drink it all.

Banana prune malt shake

Malt tastes wonderful and it's good for your digestion, so along with the prunes and banana this is certainly one to get you going in the morning. You can find malt extract in health food stores, but if you buy it from the drug store avoid the one with cod liver oil added to it—it may be good for you, but it doesn't go very well with banana!

Serves 2

2 ripe bananas

8 plump moist pitted prunes

1 tablespoon malt extract

1¼ cups whole milk

Break the bananas into a blender, then add the prunes, malt extract, and milk. Whiz until thick and frothy and drink straightaway.

Purple juice zinger

Red cabbage juice might not sound like everyone's ideal start to the day, but this is not only delicious, it's also packed with vitamins and antioxidants. When it comes to juicing, it is best to go organic and save yourself the time and energy of peeling the fruit and vegetables first.

Serves 2

1 small red cabbage, cut into large chunks

3 sweet red apples, cut into wedges

1 large knob of fresh gingerroot, peeled

Pass the cabbage, apples, and ginger through a juicer. Pour into two glasses, adding a cube or two of ice if you have any, and drink swiftly before the vitamins begin to deteriorate.

Beet purifier

Beet juice is fantastic—as well as being vitamin- and mineral-packed, it is very cleansing and can help alleviate many ailments, including bladder, kidney, and liver disorders and constipation. It is also said to stimulate the metabolism and I promise you, you'll even learn to enjoy the taste. Try to drink this once a week.

Serves 1

1 small raw beet

2 pears, cut into fourths

2 celery stalks

1 lime, peeled

Scrub the beet, then trim off the end and cut it into fourths lengthwise. Pass the beet, pears, celery, and lime through a juicer and drink swiftly before the vitamins begin to deteriorate.

Pure mango slush

Apple and mango make a perfect combination.

Serves 2
1 large mango, peeled, stoned and diced
scant ½ cup pressed fresh apple juice
1 large glass of ice

Place the mango, apple juice, and ice in a blender and whiz together until smooth and slushy. Pour into glasses and serve.

Breakfast in a glass (and a half!)

This super smoothie takes a couple of minutes to whiz up, but contains so much goodness it'll keep you going right through to lunch.

Serves 1
9 oz/250 g mixed berries such as strawberries, blueberries, and blackberries
1 small knob of fresh gingerroot, peeled and chopped
⅔ cup pressed fresh apple juice
a small handful of oatmeal
5 oz/150 g plain yogurt
1–2 tablespoons clear honey

1 Place the berries and ginger in a blender and whiz until smooth.

2 Add the apple juice, oatmeal, yogurt, and honey and whiz until frothy. Pour into a very large glass (it makes about scant 2 cups) and drink.

little fillers

Hellfire chicken wings

I just can't write a book without including a recipe for chicken wings, as I'm such a fan. Lately, though, it seems chicken wings have been downgraded in the supermarket and are mass-packed as an economy product—such a shame, as the wings are surely the most enjoyable part of the chicken, although I admit not the leanest. Nowadays, I buy mine from my local butcher, who deals only in organic birds, and he charges very little for the wings, as they're less popular than they used to be—surprising, as they're always the first to disappear from the barbecue or picnic basket!

And if you are a chili addict like me, don't worry about indulging—it is said to be a tonic for many things, including sore throat, blocked sinuses, tummy ache, poor complexion, hangovers, and bad circulation. A full tablespoon of cayenne does push the chili kick quite far, so you may prefer to use 1–2 teaspoons.

Serves 4

grated rind and juice of 1 small unwaxed orange

1 tablespoon dark muscovado sugar

1 tablespoon maple syrup or clear honey

1 tablespoon cayenne

¼ teaspoon sea salt

12 large chicken wings

1 Preheat the oven to 400°F/200°C. Place the orange rind and juice in a large bowl and stir in the sugar, syrup or honey, the cayenne, and salt.

2 Add the chicken wings and turn them to coat in the mixture. If you have time, let marinate for a while; otherwise, place on a rack set over a cookie sheet and roast in the oven for 20–25 minutes, or until golden brown and very hot and sticky.

Roasted butternut and Gorgonzola purée

Squash and pumpkins all roast beautifully, but some do taste better than others. The butternut is very common and has a lovely nutty flavor and silky texture when puréed. As well as being high in fiber, pumpkins are also an excellent source of vitamin A, which is good for our eyes, skin, hair, and teeth.

Serves/makes 4

1 large butternut squash

1 tablespoon olive oil

a pinch of ground cumin

2–3 oz/50–75 g Gorgonzola or other strong blue cheese

1 Preheat the oven to 400°F/200°C. Halve the squash and scoop out and discard the seeds. Score the flesh deeply in a criss-cross pattern to help it cook evenly, then drizzle with the oil and sprinkle with the cumin. Roast in the oven for 30 minutes or so until the flesh is tender.

2 Scoop the flesh into a bowl and coarsely mash. Stir in the cheese and serve just as it's melting.

Green chile and cumin labneh

Labneh is a traditional Lebanese soft cheese made from sheep or goat milk. My cheats' version is made from strained plain yogurt and still has a gorgeous twang to it, but by all means try making it with sheep or goats' milk yogurt, too.

1 Add the salt to the yogurt and stir together. Place a square of cheesecloth (I use a baby's cloth) in a bowl and spoon in the yogurt. Gather the ends together and tie firmly with string. Suspend the yogurt above a sink or deep bowl (I normally tie the string to a wooden spoon and suspend it over a large pitcher) and let stand overnight in a cool room.

2 Next morning, the excess liquid will have dripped out and you will be left with a firm, soft cheese in the cloth. Transfer the cheese to a bowl and stir in the chile and cumin seeds. Drizzle the surface with the oil and chill until ready to eat. It will keep in the refrigerator for up to three days. Serve with pita or breadsticks.

Serves 6

½ teaspoon sea salt

500 g/1 lb 2 oz strained plain yogurt

1 green chile, seeded and finely chopped

1 teaspoon toasted cumin seeds

1 teaspoon extra virgin olive oil

warm pita or breadsticks, to serve

Romano croutons

Romano is a Parmesan-style cheese made from sheeps' milk. Like Parmesan, it can be used at varying levels of maturity, but mostly in the U.S. we get it when it's quite hard and mature and good for grating. When I was a kid, my mom used to age huge wheels of it on a specially built shelf in the shed at home and used it so heavy-handedly in her cooking that it is only in recent years that I have finally learned to love it.

I use a flavored focaccia, such as one with rosemary or olives in it, for this recipe, as the texture and olive oil content makes for a good crunchy result. Great for dipping!

Makes/serves 6

14 oz/400 g flavored focaccia loaf, cut into cubes

a large handful of fresh, finely grated romano cheese

olive oil

1   Preheat the oven to 400°F/200°C. Place the focaccia in a large bowl. Sprinkle over the romano and toss well together. The focaccia should have enough oil in it to make the cheese stick, but if not add a little splash of oil.

2   Scatter the focaccia cubes onto a large nonstick cookie sheet in a single layer. Bake in the oven for 12 minutes, or until crunchy and golden. Let cool and store in an airtight tin.

Skordalia

Skordalia is a Greek garlic and olive oil dip/side dish that is especially good with white fish and can be made in a variety of different ways. Unlike hummus and taramasalata, skordalia is rarely seen outside of restaurants, which is a shame. This recipe is potato-based, but it can be bread-based, too—Jane Grigson's version from her wonderful *Fish Book* is a gorgeous-textured, garlic mayonnaise thickened with bread crumbs and almonds.

Don't make this with a red-skinned or waxy new potato as you won't get a good result. Choose a mealy, white-skinned variety such as Maris Piper.

1 Cook the potatoes in a pan of boiling water until tender.

2 Place the garlic in a food processor with a big pinch of salt and whiz until finely chopped. Drain the potatoes well, then add to the processor with the vinegar and whiz until very smooth. Now, slowly pour in the oil to make a glossy dip. Delicious!

Serves 4–6

500 g/1 lb 2 oz white mealy potatoes, peeled and cubed

4 plump garlic cloves, peeled and cut into fourths

2 tablespoons white wine vinegar

⅔ cup extra virgin olive oil

sea salt

Lemon mozzarella crostini

Choose good bread and top-quality mozzarella and keep this simple.

1 Drain the mozzarella and tear into pieces. Pop into a bowl with 1 tablespoon of the oil, the lemon rind and juice, and basil and stir well together.

2 Preheat a grill pan. Cut each slice of bread into fourths and drizzle over a little olive oil. Cook in the hot pan for a minute or so on each side, or until brown and a little charred.

3 Rub each piece of toast with the cut surface of the garlic clove and season with a little salt. Top with the mozzarella and serve while the toast is still warm.

Serves 2

4–5 oz/125–150 g ball buffalo mozzarella

2 tablespoons extra virgin olive oil or avocado oil

grated rind and juice of 1 small unwaxed lemon

a few torn fresh basil leaves

2 slices of sourdough bread

1 unpeeled garlic clove, halved

sea salt

Mr Ganoush's baba ganoush

Eggplants are my favorite vegetable and this has to be one of my favorite ways of using them. So keen am I on this dish that Baba Ganoush is, in fact, my little son's nickname ("Mr Ganoush" when he's in trouble). To be honest, he's not always very keen on eating the classic version, but this one is softened with a spoonful of strained plain yogurt and is very child-friendly. Serve with strips of warm flat bread or pita, for dipping.

1 Preheat the oven to 400°F/200°C. Pop the eggplants onto a cookie sheet and roast in the oven for 20–25 minutes, or until wrinkled and softened.

2 Split the eggplants open (be careful of the steam) and scoop the flesh into a food processor along with the garlic, cumin, and yogurt. Whiz until smooth.

3 Stir in the mint, then add the citrus juice and salt, to taste. Will keep in the refrigerator for 2–3 days.

Serves 4–6

2 eggplants

1 garlic clove, peeled and crushed

1 teaspoon ground cumin

2–3 tablespoons strained plain yogurt

2 tablespoons finely chopped fresh mint

a squeeze of fresh lemon or lime juice

sea salt

Soft lima bean pâté

Lima beans are very underused, if you ask me. They have such a lovely soft texture when puréed, which makes them great for pâtés and spreads. Warmed, mashed lima beans, perhaps with a little cheese melted in, make a great alternative to mashed potatoes.

1 Place the beans in a food processor and whiz to break them down. The mixture will be stiff so add the oil and 3–4 table-spoons of water until you get a nice smooth texture.

2 Stir in the chives and chile and add lemon juice and salt and pepper to taste. Spoon into a bowl, then drizzle over a little oil and chill until ready to serve. Will keep in the refrigerator for 2–3 days.

Serves 4–6

1 lb 13 oz/825 g canned lima beans, drained and rinsed

3 tablespoons extra virgin olive oil, plus extra for drizzling

3 tablespoons chopped fresh chives

1 fresh chile, seeded and finely chopped

juice of ½ lemon

sea salt and freshly ground black pepper

Red bell pepper pesto

This is a very useful little sauce—great for spreading on bruschetta, dipping grissini or croutons into (try with Romano croutons on page 30) or tossing with hot pasta.

1 Cook the red bell peppers under a hot broiler for 15–20 minutes, or until blackened and blistered all over. Place in a bowl and cover with a dish towel—the steam will soften the skin and make them easier to peel.

2 Scatter the nuts on a cookie sheet. Lower the heat of the broiler to medium and toast them for a few minutes, or until golden brown. Let cool a little, while you peel and seed the bell peppers.

3 Place the skinned bell peppers, almonds, and garlic in a food processor and whiz until as smooth as possible. Mix in the chili flakes, vinegar, and oil and season generously. Cover and chill for up to 2 days.

Serves 4

2 large red bell peppers

⅓ cup blanched almonds

1 garlic clove, peeled

a large pinch of crushed chili flakes

1 teaspoon balsamic vinegar

2 tablespoons extra virgin olive oil

sea salt and freshly ground black pepper

Simple smoked mackerel spread

Mackerel is the kind of oily fish we should all be eating at least twice a week. It's loaded with heart-friendly omega oils and the smoked varieties are easy to turn into delicious spreads. Good for salads and sandwiches.

Serves 4–6

10 oz/275 g smoked mackerel fillets

½ cup soft cheese

a few shakes of Tabasco or other chili sauce

a squeeze of fresh lemon or lime juice

2 scallions, chopped

freshly ground black pepper

1 Skin the mackerel fillets and lift out and discard the dark flesh that runs down the back of each fillet—this is the blood line and can taste bitter.

2 Break the fish into a bowl, then add the soft cheese and, using a fork, mash together. Add the chili, citrus juice, and scallions and season with black pepper. Cover and chill for up to 3 days.

Beet hummus

Couldn't be easier (or packed with many more vitamins, fiber, and antioxidants)!

Serves 4

2 cooked vacuum-packed beet

14 oz/400 g canned chickpeas, drained

1 shallot, peeled and finely chopped

3 tablespoons chopped fresh parsley

1 small garlic clove, peeled and crushed

1 tablespoon wine vinegar

2 tablespoons olive oil

sea salt and freshly ground black pepper

1 Put the beet and chickpeas in a food processor and whiz until as smooth as possible.

2 Stir in the shallot, parsley, garlic, vinegar, and oil and season to taste. Chill until ready to eat. Will keep in the refrigerator for up to 2 days.

Potted Cheshire

Cheese is often thought of as unhealthy, but it is a very valuable source of calcium. These little pots are brilliant for parties and picnics. Vary the quantities depending on how much cheese you've got to use up— any crumbly cheese such as Lancashire, Caerphilly, or Wensleydale will do fine. For a French-style potted cheese, skip the pepper sauce and add a splash of brandy instead. Serve with some whole-grain toast.

Serves 4

5 oz/150 g Cheshire cheese, crumbled

¼ cup soft cheese

¼ stick unsalted butter

a few shakes of Tabasco

Whiz all the ingredients together in a food processor until well blended but still slightly textured. Spoon into small pots or ramekins and smooth the tops. Cover with plastic wrap and chill until ready to serve. Will keep in the refrigerator for up to 4 days.

Paprika'd popcorn

It's such a shame we associate popcorn only with going to the movies, when it is so easy to make at home. Popcorn is a nutritious snack that gets a bad reputation from being smothered in butter and sugar. A little oil, a bit of spice, and in a matter of minutes you've got a delicious snack that is healthier and tastier than any package of chips.

Serves 1–2

1 oz/25 g popping corn

1 teaspoon vegetable oil

1 teaspoon paprika

sea salt

1 Place the corn and oil in a large pan and cover with a lid, then set over medium-high heat. Cook for 5 minutes or so until all the popping subsides.

2 Add the paprika and some sea salt and shake the pan vigorously. Best served warm, but any leftovers can be stored for a few days in an airtight container.

Avocado and basil mayo

Did you know the avocado is listed in *The Guinness Book of Records* as the most nutritious fruit known to man? Not only is it packed with vitamins, fiber, and heart-friendly oils, the taste and texture of the avocado is just fantastic. This dip is leaning towards guacamole, but the texture is creamy and smooth like that of mayonnaise. The avocados you choose must be ripe, and I sometimes stir in a very finely chopped shallot at the last minute.

1 Place the garlic, basil, and some salt in a mini food processor and whiz until blended to a paste.

2 Add the avocados and whiz until smooth. Blend in the oil and vinegar and check the seasoning. It discolors fairly quickly so don't make this too far ahead of time. Serve at room temperature.

Serves 4–6

1 garlic clove, peeled and crushed

a large handful of fresh basil leaves

2 ripe avocados, halved, skinned, pitted and cubed

2 tablespoons avocado oil or extra virgin olive oil

2 teaspoons wine vinegar

sea salt and freshly ground black pepper

Home-spiced tortilla chips

These are very easy to make and you can vary the heat factor depending on what mood you're in. Serve with a simple tomato salsa (see below) for dipping.

1 Mix the oil with the spices and brush over the tortillas. Cut each one into 16 wedges—slice them as though you were cutting a cake.

2 Place the wedges in a single layer on a large cookie sheet. Cook under a medium broiler for 4–5 minutes, or until crisp and golden brown and maybe a touch charred at the tips. Serve warm or at room temperature.

Simple tomato salsa

Coarsely chop 1 garlic clove and 1 shallot or a scallion or two. Whiz in a mini food processor until finely minced, then add 2 coarsely chopped ripe tomatoes and a splash of olive oil and whiz again. Add salt, a squeeze of lemon juice, and any chopped herbs you have to hand.

Serves 2

1 tablespoon olive or vegetable oil

¼ teaspoon cayenne

¼ teaspoon ground cumin

¼ teaspoon ground coriander

2 soft corn tortillas

Sandwiches, wraps, and toasties

Leicester nonsense with dill pickle

I quite like Quark—it's very neutral, which means it's excellent for binding things together without interfering with their flavor too much. It is naturally low in fat and is readily available in most supermarkets. In Germany the word "quark" is used conversationally to mean "nonsense!".

1   Bring a small pan of water to a boil. Add the eggs and boil for 8 minutes, then drain them and cool under water.

2   Shell the eggs, then mash them with a fork. Stir in the cheeses, onion, and plenty of black pepper.

3   Spread some of the filling onto two slices of the bread, then lay on the sliced pickles. Top with the rest of the filling, then sandwich with the remaining two slices of bread. Squash down a bit, then cut and eat.

Serves 2

2 large eggs, at room temperature

3 oz/75 g good-quality Leicester cheese, coarsely grated

3 oz/75 g Quark or other soft cheese

1 small red onion, peeled and finely chopped

4 slices of thickly sliced whole-wheat bread, lightly buttered

2 large dill pickles, thinly sliced lengthwise

freshly ground black pepper

Crab and crispy bacon doubles

A lovely old-fashioned double decker, this is sort of an updated club sandwich. Make sure you use good quality lean bacon for a firm, crispy bite.

1 Heat a large nonstick pan and add the bacon. Cook over high heat for 3–4 minutes, or until the bacon begins to release its oils into the pan, then add the tomatoes and cook for an additional 5 minutes, or until the bacon is crispy and the tomatoes have softened.

2 Meanwhile, mix the crab with the butter, shallot, and cayenne, then add the lime juice and salt and pepper to taste.

3 Make two double-decker sandwiches using the lettuce greens, crispy bacon, and tomatoes on the bottom level and the spiced crab on the top deck. Eat warm or wrap in greaseproof paper and pack into a lunch box.

Serves 2

8 strips streaky bacon

6 cherry tomatoes, halved

6 oz/175 g canned white crab meat, drained

2 tablespoons melted butter

1 shallot, peeled and finely chopped

a pinch of cayenne

a squeeze of fresh lime juice

6 slices of soft whole-grain bread, lightly buttered

a large handful of baby lettuce greens

sea salt and freshly ground black pepper

James's Moroccan chicken wrap

This recipe has been devised by my friend James Fisher. He's a very accomplished chef, so this sandwich is a bit more complicated than most of the others in this chapter, but is definitely worth taking the extra time over.

Although there seems to be lots of fiddly bits and pieces, they all come together fantastically. For the chicken you can use leftovers from a Sunday roast or you can buy thigh and drumstick packages from most supermarkets—just roast them following the directions on the package.

1 Preheat the oven to 325°F/160°C. Slice the tomatoes in half and place cut-side up on a wire rack set on a baking sheet. Sprinkle over the garlic and some black pepper and drizzle over some of the oil. Slow-cook in the oven for 1–2 hours, or until the tomatoes have become wrinkled and are beginning to brown. You can make these the day before.

2 Place the chickpeas in a mixing bowl with the parsley, lemon juice, onion, a splash of olive oil, the cumin, and some salt and pepper and gently spoon together.

3 Vigorously mix the harissa into the mayo until it is an even pink blush color.

4 Cook the tortillas in a hot nonstick skillet for 15 seconds, or until they begin to blister.

5 To assemble, lay the tortillas on a board. Divide the chicken between them, then top with the chickpea salad, followed by the roasted tomatoes. Spoon over the harissa mayo and roll up, then eat.

Serves 4

4 ripe tomatoes

1 garlic clove, peeled and thinly sliced

2 tablespoons olive oil

14 oz/400 g canned chickpeas, drained

1 small bunch of fresh parsley, coarsely chopped

juice of 1 lemon

1 red onion, peeled and thinly sliced

½ teaspoon ground cumin

1 teaspoon harissa paste

4 tablespoons mayonnaise

4 flour tortillas

14 oz/400 g roasted chicken, shredded

sea salt and freshly ground black pepper

Wasabi beef and cucumber rolls

This is a very good sandwich if you're not feeling too perky or are suffering the effects of a big night out—the flavors are very lively, it's not too heavy on the carbs, and the wasabi is a real head-clearer.

I like to make these using the sort of pancakes you normally use with crispy Peking duck. In the supermarket they are usually stocked in the refrigerator near the duck. You can use flour tortillas, but they are rather bready.

1 Place the steak in a shallow dish and rub in the soy sauce and sake or sherry. Let marinate for 10 minutes to 2 hours.

2 Preheat a grill pan. Scatter the sugar over the steak, pressing it in with your fingertips and, once the pan is really hot, cook for a couple of minutes on each side until nicely browned but still a little pink in the center.

3 Let the steak rest for 5 minutes, then cut into ½ inch/1 cm thick strips. If you're going to eat the rolls immediately, use the steak while still warm; otherwise, let it cool completely before rolling.

4 Smear the pancakes or tortillas with wasabi and then roll up with the cucumber, arugula, and steak.

Serves 2

1 large trimmed sirloin or rump steak, about 9 oz/250 g

1 tablespoon soy sauce

1 tablespoon sake or dry sherry

1 tablespoon light muscovado or other brown sugar

4 pancakes or 2 flour tortillas

1–2 teaspoons wasabi paste

2½ inch/6 cm piece of cucumber, sliced or cut into short thin sticks

a bowl of fresh arugula

Ham on rye with mustard and watercress

Dark rye bread can be a bit overwhelming, so go for a light rye that contains a mix of white and rye flours and ideally some rye seeds, too. The flavor combination of rye, ham, and mustard is a long-time classic.

Serves 2

1 tablespoon clear honey

1 tablespoon whole-grain mustard

2 thick slices of baked ham

4 slices of lightly buttered rye bread

a handful of watercress

a few shakes of balsamic vinegar

1 Mix the honey with the mustard.

2 Place the ham on two slices of bread, then top with the watercress. Drizzle over the honey and mustard and splash over a little balsamic vinegar. Sandwich with the remaining slices of bread.

Smoked salmon and salsa verde bagels

A mini-chopper makes very light work of this salsa verde, which will keep in the refrigerator for a few days and is also good with most cheese and cold meats.

Serves 4

1 scallion, coarsely chopped

1 large gherkin, coarsely chopped

2 teaspoons capers, rinsed

1 large bunch of fresh parsley

1 small bunch of fresh mint or cilantro

4 tablespoons olive oil

juice of 1 lemon

4 whole-grain bagels

7 oz/200 g smoked salmon

sea salt and freshly ground black pepper

1 Place the scallion, gherkin, capers, parsley, and mint or cilantro in a food processor and whiz until chopped and well blended. Add the oil and lemon juice, and some salt and black pepper, then whiz again to make a coarse paste.

2 Split each bagel and lightly toast the cut sides. Fold the salmon slices over the bases. Spoon over the salsa verde and top with the bagel halves.

Great gravlax sandwich

Soft cheese and boiled eggs make perfect companions to cured and smoked fish, cutting through the salty flavor and oily texture perfectly. Given the choice, I go down the Scandinavian route and choose a light rye bread for this sandwich, but if you can't get it, whole-grain is okay, too. If you want to carry on with the Scandinavian theme, serve this as an open sandwich, smorgasbord style.

1 Bring a small pan of water to a boil. Add the eggs and boil for 8 minutes, then drain them and cool under water.

2 Slice the cucumber and place in a bowl with the lemon juice or vinegar and the herbs, separating the slices so the liquid and herbs mingle.

3 Spread the cheese onto two of the slices of bread and top with the gravlax or smoked salmon. Shell and slice the eggs and arrange on top of the fish along with the cucumber, then grind over some pepper.

4 For a closed sandwich, lightly butter the remaining two slices of bread and press down on top, otherwise serve open.

Serves 2

2 large eggs, at room temperature

¼ cucumber

juice of ½ lemon or 1 tablespoon wine vinegar

1–2 tablespoons fresh dill leaves or shredded fresh basil leaves

scant ½ cup soft cheese

2 or 4 slices of bread

4 oz/125 g package gravlax or smoked salmon

a small knob of butter, at room temperature (optional)

freshly ground black pepper

Tuna cobs

In my home town of Derby, England, we call crusty round bread rolls "cobs," because of their resemblance to the street cobbles. Everywhere else though, they just seem to be called crusty bread rolls, which is not quite as descriptive. Anyway, tuna is a classic filler, but really needs to be paired with something that has a bit of bite and maybe a touch of sweetness—in this case we're using apple. This is a very useful filling and is also great in baked potatoes and crêpes.

1 Core and chop the apple, then cut into fourths, but leave the skin on. Mix with the tuna, scallions, yogurt, seeds, a squeeze of fresh lime juice, and some salt and plenty of black pepper.

2 Split and fill the cobs, wrap in waxed paper and pack into a lunch box.

Serves 2

1 red apple

7 oz/200 g canned tuna fillets in spring water, drained

4 scallions, sliced

4 tablespoons strained plain yogurt

1 teaspoon onion seeds or sesame seeds

a squeeze of fresh lime juice

2 cobs

sea salt and freshly ground black pepper

Gruyère and balsamic onion toasties

Most supermarkets stock those jars of gorgeous marinated baby onions and they are just wonderful with cheese. They are, however, pretty pricey and it's easy to make your own balsamic onions at home—I guess it just depends on what you've got in the cupboard and how much time you have.

1 Spread one side of each slice of bread with butter. Divide the cheese and onions between two unbuttered sides and top with the remaining bread, unbuttered side down.

2 Place the sandwiches in a large nonstick skillet. Turn on the heat—it's a good idea to start heating slowly, otherwise the bread will crisp up before the cheese gets a chance to melt.

3 Cook for a few minutes on each side until the cheese is bubbling around the edges and the bread is crisp and golden. Slide each sandwich onto a plate, then cut in half and eat while still warm.

Balsamic onions

Heat 1 spoonful of olive or vegetable oil in a small skillet and cook 1 sliced onion for a few minutes until beginning to soften and turn golden. If you have any yellow mustard seeds, sprinkle in a few. Now add 1 teaspoon superfine sugar and 1 tablespoon balsamic vinegar and cook very gently for an additional 5 minutes. If you have any herbs, such as thyme, rosemary, or parsley, chop them and add to the onions, then cook for a minute or two more. Season with sea salt and freshly ground black pepper.

Serves 2

4 slices of mixed grain country bread

a knob of butter

3½ oz/100 g Gruyère or Emmenthal cheese, thinly sliced or grated

balsamic onions (see below) or 4 marinated onions from jar, sliced

Avocado and havarti toasted tortillas

Havarti is a lovely buttery-tasting, semihard cheese that melts brilliantly. I wouldn't normally pair avocado with cheese and certainly not a Danish one, but it just works so well here.

1 Scoop the avocado out of its shell and cube the flesh. Using a fork, flatten the avocado onto one of the tortillas. Scatter over the cheese and basil and then add some chili sauce and lime juice and a few good grinds of black pepper.

2 Sandwich the other tortilla on top, then place in a large nonstick skillet. Turn on the heat—it's a good idea to start heating slowly, otherwise the tortilla will crisp up before the cheese gets a chance to melt.

3 Cook for a few minutes on each side until the cheese is bubbling around the edges and the bread is crisp and golden. Slide the tortilla onto a plate, then cut into wedges and eat while still warm.

Serves 1

1 small or ½ avocado

2 flour tortillas

1½ oz/40 g havarti cheese, diced

a few fresh basil leaves

a few shakes of Tabasco or other chili sauce

a squeeze of fresh lime juice

freshly ground black pepper

Rice paper shrimp and glass noodle rolls

These delicate little rolls do take a bit of patience to assemble, but they're great for a special occasion or if you fancy showing off your packed lunch at work. Glass or cellophane noodles are usually made from bean starch and when reconstituted are clear, but vermicelli rice noodles, which are not translucent, make a good substitute and are readily available in supermarkets. Make sure you get all the ingredients prepared before you begin to roll.

1 Place the noodles in a large heatproof bowl. Cover with a kettleful of boiling water and set aside for a few minutes until softened, then drain and cool.

2 Fill a large heatproof bowl with hot water. Submerge one rice paper skin in the water and soak it for about 1 minute, or until softened. Carefully remove the rice paper from the water and lay it flat on a clean towel.

3 Place a few noodles, 2 shrimp, and a sprinkling of scallions, ginger, sesame seeds, and cilantro leaves horizontally across the center of the skin. Fold over the left and right edges of the skin to enclose the ends of the filling and then, starting at the bottom, roll up to completely enclose the filling and form a neat cylinder. Repeat to use up all the skins and the filling. You may need to replace the hot water if it cools down too much. Chill the rolls, join-side down, until ready to eat.

Dipping sauce

These rolls are often accompanied by a dipping sauce.
Mix your own blend or mix 2 tablespoons light soy sauce with 1 tablespoon water, 1 teaspoon rice or wine vinegar, and ½ teaspoon Asian chili oil.

Serves 4

2 oz/50 g glass or vermicelli rice noodles

16 x 9 inch/23 cm round rice paper skins

9 oz/250 g cooked shelled jumbo shrimp (you'll need 32 in total)

6 scallions, shredded

1 tablespoon chopped pickled ginger

2 teaspoons sesame seeds

a handful of fresh cilantro leaves

dipping sauce, to serve (see below)

Spiced chicken chapattis

I'm cooking the chicken from fresh, but if you're in a hurry you can use marinated cooked chicken fillets from the supermarket. Chapattis are a good alternative to flour tortillas, as they tend to be made using a good proportion of whole-wheat flour.

1 Preheat the broiler to medium. In a shallow bowl, mix half the yogurt with the curry paste, seeds, and some salt and pepper. Dip the chicken in the yogurt mixture to coat it completely. Broil for 6–8 minutes on each side, or until nicely browned and cooked through. Let cool.

2 Meanwhile, place the garlic, mint, and remaining yogurt in a mini food processor and whiz until the mint is finely chopped in—or you can use a hand-held blender. Add a squeeze of one of the lemon wedges and salt and pepper to taste.

3 Pile the lettuce onto the chapattis. Slice the chicken and arrange on top, then drizzle over the minty yogurt. Fold in half or roll up and eat.

Serves 2

5 oz/150 g plain yogurt

1 tablespoon curry paste

¼ teaspoon mustard seeds

¼ teaspoon cumin seeds

2 small skinless boneless chicken breasts

1 small garlic clove, peeled

1 bunch of fresh mint

1 lemon, cut into wedges

1 Boston lettuce, shredded

2 chapattis

sea salt and freshly ground black pepper

Simple salad sandwich

I don't know about you, but sometimes I just want a simple salad sandwich. This is the best one I know.

1 Mix the carrot with the scallion, linseeds, a good squeeze of lemon juice, and some salt and pepper.

2 Arrange the spinach or arugula leaves and the tomato on one slice of the bread, then pile on the carrot mixture. Scatter the sprouts on top. Sandwich with the remaining slice and serve.

Serves 1

1 carrot, peeled and coarsely grated

1 scallion, shredded

1 teaspoon linseeds

a squeeze of fresh lemon juice

a large handful of baby spinach or arugula leaves

1 firm tomato, sliced

2 slices of whole-grain bread, lightly spread with mayonnaise

a large handful of mustard and cress or alfalfa sprouts

sea salt and freshly ground black pepper

Real falafel with flat breads

Some of you may argue that falafel are actually deep-fried fast food and there is a point to that argument because, yes, they are indeed fried. But, they taste so wonderful I could never give them up. And they are made almost entirely of chickpeas, which contain phytochemicals called saponins, which act as antioxidants. They can help to lower cholesterol levels and are also a good source of protein and fiber. And this is the only deep-fried recipe in the book!

Real falafel are made using dried chickpeas, which have to be soaked overnight and so makes them appear time-consuming, but really they're so simple—just put the chickpeas in to soak before you go to bed.

1 To make the falafel, place all the ingredients except the sunflower-seed oil in a food processor and whiz to a rough purée.

2 Using your hands, very firmly shape the mixture into 30 balls, then pat each one into a little cake. If the mixture starts to stick, dampen your hands with water. Be firm, or the cakes may break during frying. If you have time now, chill them for a while.

3 Heat sufficient oil for deep-frying in a deep pan and when it is hot enough to brown a cube of bread in about 30 seconds, cook the falafel in batches for 4–5 minutes, or until crunchy and dark brown. Drain on paper towels, then serve with flat breads and salad.

To serve
Flat breads or pita and salad (try Minted coleslaw on page 116, or Mr Ganoush's baba ganoush on page 34).

Serves 6

8 oz/225 g dried chickpeas, soaked overnight in water

1 small red onion, peeled and finely chopped

2 tablespoons chopped fresh parsley

2 garlic cloves, peeled and finely chopped

1 teaspoon cumin seeds

½ teaspoon ground cumin

1 teaspoon ground coriander

1 teaspoon baking powder

juice of 1 lime

sea salt and freshly ground black pepper

sunflower-seed oil, for deep-frying

SOUPS

Mushroom and rice soup with goat cheese

I was going to call this a congee, which is a Chinese rice soup, but it's actually a bit more like a very soft risotto. I'm using basmati rice, but it will work with any type of white rice.

1 Place the dried mushrooms in a large pitcher and pour over the hot stock. Set aside for 10 minutes.

2 Heat the oil in a large pan and cook the onion, garlic, and thyme for 5 minutes, or until softened. Add the chopped fresh mushrooms and cook for an additional 5 minutes. Add the rice, then strain in the stock and bring to a boil.

3 Meanwhile, chop the rehydrated dried mushrooms and stir into the pan. Reduce the heat and simmer, uncovered, for 40 minutes.

4 Add salt and pepper to taste, then ladle into bowls. Cut the cheese into fourths and drop a piece into each bowl. Grind over some more black pepper and serve.

Serves 4

½ oz/15 g dried mushrooms

8 cups hot vegetable stock

1 tablespoon olive oil

1 small onion, peeled and finely chopped

2 garlic cloves, peeled and finely chopped

2 fresh thyme sprigs

1 lb/450 g portabella mushrooms, chopped

½ cup basmati rice

3½ oz/100 g round firm goat cheese

sea salt and freshly ground black pepper

Cannellini bean soup with a little bit of chorizo

Chorizo is not what you'd call a naturally healthy ingredient, but it is absolutely full of flavor and this recipe calls for only a small amount, so all in all this is very balanced, nutritious and delicious. Make sure you buy a nice chunk of chorizo sausage from the deli counter, rather than the pre-sliced packet sort.

1 Heat the oil in a large pan and cook the onion and garlic for 10 minutes, or until lightly browned. Add the cannellini beans and the water and bring to a boil.

2 Take off the heat and, using a hand-held blender, blitz the soup until creamy but not completely smooth. Return to the heat and simmer for 5 minutes.

3 Meanwhile, cook the diced chorizo in a nonstick skillet for 5 minutes, or until it begins to crisp up and release its lovely paprika oil.

4 Stir the spinach into the soup and cook for a minute or two until wilted. Season with salt and pepper, then stir in most of the chorizo and its oils, saving a few bits to decorate the top of each bowl.

Serves 4

1 tablespoon olive oil

1 onion, peeled and chopped

4 garlic cloves, peeled and chopped

1 lb 12 oz/800 g canned cannellini beans, drained

3½ cups water

3½ oz/100 g chorizo sausage, finely diced

1 lb 2 oz/500 g young spinach greens

sea salt and freshly ground black pepper

Bourride

A classic French fish soup is one of the most enjoyable lunches I could imagine. This one is usually served with cheesy toasts floating on the surface and sometimes a good dollop of chili-mayonnaise. This version contains potatoes, so it'll fill you up just fine without the need for toast. Or cheese. Although, of course, if you are feeling extra hungry…

1 Heat the oil in a very large pan and cook the onion and garlic for 5 minutes, or until softened. Add the saffron and wine, then bring to a boil and bubble rapidly for 5 minutes. Dissolve the stock cube in the boiling water and add to the pan along with the potatoes and tomatoes. Bring to a boil, then reduce the heat and simmer gently for 20 minutes.

2 Add the mussels to the pan, then cover with a lid and cook for 3 minutes. Add the fish and shrimp to the pan and cook for 2 minutes.

3 Check that the stew is piping hot and the fish is cooked through. Discard any mussels that haven't opened. Stir in the parsley and plenty of black pepper, then ladle into large bowls and serve.

Serves 6

1 tablespoon olive oil

1 onion, peeled and coarsely chopped

2 garlic cloves, cut into fourths

a pinch of saffron

generous ¾ cup dry white wine

1 chicken stock cube

3 cups boiling water

2 white potatoes, peeled and cubed

4 fresh, ripe tomatoes, coarsely chopped

2¼ lb/1 kg live mussels, scrubbed and bearded

1 lb 2 oz/500 g white fish, such as cod or haddock, cut into good-size cubes

14 oz/400 g raw jumbo shrimp, unshelled

4 tablespoons chopped fresh parsley

freshly ground black pepper

Five-minute chicken miso soup

Miso is a protein-rich paste made from fermented soy beans. It has a delicious savory flavor and contains enzymes that are very good for digestion. Buy it in Asian stores or from health food stores.

1 Place the noodles in a heatproof bowl and cover with a kettleful of boiling water—they are meant to be "straight to wok," but boiling water loosens the noodles and stops them sticking to each other or breaking.

2 Pour the 5 cups boiling water into a large pan and stir in the mushrooms, bok choy, chicken, and miso paste. Cook gently for 3–4 minutes without boiling, or until the vegetables are tender.

3 Drain the noodles and divide between bowls. Ladle over the miso soup and vegetables. Scatter over the chile and scallions and serve.

Serves 4

5 oz/150 g package thin "straight-to-wok" (precooked) noodles

5 cups boiling water, plus a kettleful

9 oz/250 g shiitake mushrooms, sliced

6 small bok choy, halved

9 oz/250 g cooked chicken, torn into bite-size pieces

3 tablespoons miso paste

1 red chile, thinly sliced, seeds and all

4 scallions, thinly sliced

Ham and parsley soup

This is a very economical but substantial and fantastic-tasting soup. Ask your butcher for the meat—it doesn't really matter if yours is a bit smaller or larger, but a lot of the flavor comes from the bone so that bit is essential, and be really generous with the parsley.

This takes a long time to simmer, but is very simple. It will freeze well in those handy "pour and store" food bags. Serve with crusty bread.

1 Heat the butter in a large pan and cook the leeks, potatoes, and rosemary for 5 minutes. Add the ham and water. Bring to a boil, then half cover the pan and reduce the heat, and simmer for 1½ hours.

2 Take the pan off the heat and lift out the ham and rosemary stems. Whiz the soup until smooth with a hand-held blender. Cut the skin and fat off the meat, then, using two forks, shred the ham from the bone (or chop it with a knife if you find it easier) and stir back into the soup—at this stage you can cool and freeze the soup.

3 Stir in the sour cream and season with lots of black pepper. Once piping hot, mix in the parsley and serve the soup with crusty bread.

Serves 6

a large knob of unsalted butter

2 large leeks, sliced

2 large white potatoes, about 1 lb/450 g, peeled and cubed

2 rosemary stems

2¼–2½ lb/1–1.25 kg bone-in bacon or ham joint, such as hock or knuckle

generous 2½ quarts/2.5 liters water

⅔ cup sour cream

1 large bunch of fresh parsley, chopped

freshly ground black pepper

Pea and lemon soup with feta

Peas in any form are perfect for making soup. This one calls for regular green peas and I normally just use frozen—especially the sweet little petits pois. Following on from the record-breaking avocado, peas must rank very highly in terms of nutritious foods—they are among the best vegetable sources of fiber and protein and also contain vitamin C, iron, and zinc.

1 Heat the oil in a large pan and cook the onion, chile, and garlic for 5 minutes, or until softened.

2 Add the peas, lettuce greens, and hot stock and bring to a boil, then reduce the heat and simmer for 5 minutes, or until the peas are tender.

3 Take off the heat and, using a hand-held blender, coarsely blitz until coarsely puréed. Stir in the lemon rind and juice and season with salt and plenty of black pepper.

4 Ladle into bowls and scatter over the feta and mint leaves.

Serves 4

2 tablespoons olive oil

1 onion, peeled and coarsely chopped

1 red chile, seeded and coarsely chopped

4 garlic cloves, peeled and coarsely chopped

1 lb 10 oz/800 g peas

1 small round lettuce, leaves separated and washed

4 cups hot chicken or vegetable stock

grated rind and juice of 1 unwaxed lemon

3 oz/75 g feta cheese, crumbled into small pieces

a few fresh mint leaves

sea salt and freshly ground black pepper

Turkish mint soup

This is a really simple soup but the combined flavor of the mint and yogurt is just lovely. Yogurt can curdle if it gets too hot, so make sure you take the pan off the heat before you add it and don't reheat it. If you have leftovers, serve them chilled.

1   Heat the butter in a large pan and cook the garlic and onion for 5 minutes, or until softened. Stir in the zucchini and cook for an additional 5 minutes.

2   Pour in the hot stock and bring to a boil, then reduce the heat and simmer for 10 minutes, or until the zucchini are tender. Stir in the mint and take off the heat, then, using a hand-held blender, whiz until completely smooth.

3   Stir the yogurt into the soup and season with salt and pepper. Serve warm, or cool and serve chilled.

Serves 4

a small knob of butter

1 garlic clove, peeled and chopped

1 small onion, peeled and chopped

4 zucchini, about 1½ lb/750 g, sliced

3 cups hot chicken or vegetable stock

1 large bunch of fresh mint leaves, coarsely chopped

1 lb 2 oz/500 g strained plain yogurt

sea salt and freshly ground black pepper

Carrot and lime soup

Carrot always makes a lovely soup. It's naturally quite a sweet vegetable, so I always either bring out its natural sweetness with, say, fresh orange, or, as in this case, cut against it with lime juice. Choose organic carrots and scrub rather than peel them for maximum vitamin content. Oh, and no added fat in this one!

1 Place the carrots, potato, onion, garlic, and hot stock in a large pan. Bring to a boil, then reduce the heat and simmer gently for 20 minutes.

2 Take off the heat and, using a hand-held blender, whiz the soup until smooth. Season with salt and pepper, then stir in the lime juice and cilantro.

3 To serve, ladle the soup into bowls and sprinkle with cumin seeds.

Serves 4

4 large carrots, grated

1 large white potato, scrubbed and grated

1 onion, peeled and finely chopped

2 garlic cloves, peeled and chopped

6¼ cups hot vegetable stock

juice of 2 limes

2 tablespoons chopped fresh cilantro

1 teaspoon toasted cumin seeds

sea salt and freshly ground black pepper

Summer bread soup

This is essentially a fresh tomato soup and is really only worth making in the summer when the tomatoes are sweet and ripe. It is designed to be served chilled (take to work in your flask to keep it cool), but you can warm it up if you really want to.

1   Using either a heavy knife or a pestle and mortar, crush the garlic with some salt to make a smooth paste.

2   Place the tomatoes, cucumber, chile, bread, and garlic paste in a food processor and whiz until smooth. If you object to the tomato skin and seeds, pass the mixture through a strainer, otherwise tip into a large bowl.

3   Stir in the water, oil, vinegar, and sugar, then add salt and pepper to taste. Chill until ready to eat.

4   To serve, chop or coarsely tear the prosciutto into pieces and ladle the soup into bowls. Scatter over the prosciutto and a few extra drops of olive oil and enjoy.

Serves 4

2 garlic cloves, peeled

2¼ lb/1 kg ripe tomatoes

4 inch/10 cm piece of cucumber, peeled and cubed

1 red chile, seeded and coarsely chopped

3½ oz/100 g crustless white bread

3 cups water

4 tablespoons extra virgin olive oil

2 tablespoons red wine vinegar

1 teaspoon superfine sugar

2 slices of prosciutto

flaky sea salt and freshly ground black pepper

Italian lentil and pasta soup

I've been making this soup ever since I first learned to cook. It's warm, delicious, and cheap and saw me right through my college days. The combination of pasta and lentils makes a very nutritious balance indeed—protein, carbs, fiber, vitamins, and plenty of flavor in every bowlful. The bacon is nice but not essential.

1 Heat the oil in a large pan and cook the onion, garlic, celery, carrot, and bacon for 5–8 minutes, or until the onion has softened. Stir in the rosemary, lentils, and tomato and cook for a couple of minutes more.

2 Stir in the hot water and simmer, uncovered, for 20–30 minutes, or until the lentils are tender and the liquid is quite reduced. Cook them for longer if you have time—it's best when the lentils start to break down a little.

3 Cook the pasta in a separate pan of boiling water according to the package directions. Drain and stir into the cooked lentils. Check the seasoning and serve. (This isn't as good when left to cool and reheated the next day, as the pasta tends to absorb the liquid if left for a few hours, so make sure you eat it all at once.)

Serves 4

2 tablespoons olive oil

1 onion, peeled and finely chopped

2 garlic cloves, peeled and finely chopped

1 celery stalk, finely chopped

1 carrot, peeled and finely chopped

1–2 strips lean bacon, chopped

1 fresh rosemary or thyme stem

1 cup dried green or brown lentils

1 ripe tomato, coarsely chopped

4 cups hot water

3 oz/75 g small pasta shapes (tubetti are my favorite for this)

sea salt and freshly ground black pepper

Moroccan-spiced red onion soup

I subscribe to a weekly organic vegetable box scheme and always seem to have tons of onions left over at the end of the month, but this is the perfect way to use them up—you can use regular brown onions, too, if you've got them. I guess it's a spin on the classic French onion soup and, as such, is quite light.

1 Heat the oil in a large pan and gently cook the onions for 15 minutes, or until golden and softened.

2 Add the cumin and cinnamon and cook for an additional 5 minutes, then add the hot stock and simmer for 10 minutes.

3 Meanwhile, brush the bread with the oil and sprinkle with the paprika. Pop under a low broiler for 8 minutes or so until golden and crispy—if using pita, split them in half first.

4 Stir the orange rind and juice and the parsley into the soup, then ladle into bowls. Break the crispy bread into pieces and scatter over the soup. Serve swiftly.

Serves 4

2 tablespoons vegetable oil

6 red onions, peeled and sliced

1 teaspoon cumin seeds

2 cinnamon sticks

6¼ cups hot chicken stock

grated rind and juice of 1 large unwaxed orange

2 tablespoons chopped fresh parsley

To serve

1 large flat bread or 2 pitas

1 teaspoon vegetable oil

1 teaspoon smoked paprika

Chile cornmeal soup

This is a sort of Mexican hotchpotch using all the obvious ingredients, but made interesting with the added cornmeal to give it some body. It'll make you feel happy and sunny on a cold, wet evening. If you're feeling really fed up, leave out the lime and stir a handful of grated cheese into each bowlful—comfort food at its best.

1 Heat the oil in a pan and cook the onion, garlic, and half the chopped chiles for 5 minutes, or until softened. Add the chili powder and cook for 1 minute more.

2 Stir in the cornmeal or polenta, the tomatoes, beans and stock. Bring to a boil, stirring from time to time, then reduce the heat and simmer gently for 20 minutes.

3 Season the soup and add the lime rind and juice to taste. Ladle into bowls and top each with some of the remaining green chiles and the cilantro leaves.

Serves 4

1 tablespoon olive oil

1 onion, peeled and chopped

2 garlic cloves, peeled and chopped

4 green chiles, seeded and chopped

1–2 teaspoons hot chili powder

2 oz/50 g cornmeal or polenta

14 oz/400 g canned chopped plum tomatoes

14 oz/400 g canned kidney beans, drained

6¼ cups hot vegetable stock

grated rind and juice of 1 unwaxed lime

a handful of fresh cilantro leaves

sea salt and freshly ground black pepper

Chickpea purée with crispy shallots

I love chickpeas and they love us, too. They're an excellent source of protein, fiber, and vitamins and taste lovely, especially in this soft smooth soup.

1 Heat the olive oil in a large pan and cook the onion and garlic for 5 minutes, or until they start to turn translucent. Add the cumin seeds and the harissa paste and cook for another minute, then add the chickpeas, potato, and water. Bring to a boil, then reduce the heat and simmer gently for 30 minutes.

2 For the crispy onions, separate the shallot slices onto a double layer of paper towels and sprinkle with salt. Heat 1 cm/½ inch of vegetable oil in a large skillet until hot, then pat the onions dry with the paper and cook for a few minutes until brown and crispy. Drain with a slotted spoon and place on paper towels to absorb any excess oil.

3 Using a hand-held blender, whiz the soup until smooth. At this point, you can set the soup aside for serving later if you want to. When ready to eat, warm the soup through, but do not boil again. Stir through the yogurt and cilantro, then add salt and pepper to taste and serve, or whiz again to blend in the herb.

4 Ladle into bowls. Sprinkle over the crispy shallots and serve.

Serves 4

1 tablespoon olive oil

1 onion, peeled and coarsely chopped

3 garlic cloves, peeled and coarsely chopped

1 teaspoon cumin seeds

2–3 teaspoons harissa paste or other chili sauce

1 lb 12 oz/800 g canned chickpeas, drained

1 white potato, peeled and diced

6¼ cups water

⅔ cup strained plain yogurt

1 bunch of fresh cilantro, chopped

sea salt and freshly ground black pepper

For the crispy shallots

4 shallots, peeled and thinly sliced

sea salt

vegetable oil, for shallow-frying

Simple roasted tomato soup

Roasted tomato soup is a modern classic. It is by far the best way to make a tomato soup, as the roasting process really intensifies and sweetens the flavor.

1 Preheat the oven to 350°F/180°C. Place the tomatoes and garlic in a roasting pan. Scatter over the basil and drizzle over the olive oil. Season and roast for 40–50 minutes, or until the tomatoes are softened and a little charred. Take the garlic out of the pan if it starts to get too dark—much past dark golden— as it can taste a little bitter.

2 Meanwhile, place the stock and potatoes in a large pan. Bring to a boil, then cover and simmer for 15–20 minutes, or until tender.

3 Slip the garlic out of its papery skin and add to the pan, along with the tomatoes and basil. Using a hand-held blender, whiz until thick and fairly smooth.

4 Season to taste then ladle into bowls and serve scattered with Romano croutons.

Serves 4

2¼ lb/1 kg ripe tomatoes, halved

1 head of garlic, halved horizontally

a handful of fresh basil leaves

2 tablespoons olive oil

6¼ cups vegetable stock

1 white potato, peeled and diced

sea salt and freshly ground black pepper

Romano croutons (page 30), to serve

Simple Thai chicken soup

You can make this in about 20 minutes. It uses only super-market ingredients and is bursting with flavor!

1 Place the noodles in a heatproof bowl and pour over a kettleful of boiling water.

2 Put half the chiles, the ginger, and hot stock in a large pan. Lightly flatten the lemon grass stalk and add to the pan. Bring to a boil, then reduce the heat and simmer gently for 5–10 minutes.

3 Add the chicken, coconut cream, and mushrooms and simmer for 3 minutes. Add the bok choy and simmer for an additional 2 minutes.

4 Drain the noodles and divide between bowls. Top each pile of noodles with a handful of bean sprouts.

5 Season the soup with the lime juice and fish sauce, if using, then ladle into the bowls. Scatter over the scallions and the remaining chiles and serve hot.

Serves 4

4 oz/100 g flat rice noodles

3 hot red chiles, seeded and finely chopped

1 large knob of fresh gingerroot, peeled and shredded

6¼ cups hot chicken stock

1 lemon grass stalk

2 large skinless, boneless chicken breasts, cut into strips

7 oz/200 g coconut cream

7 oz/200 g shiitake or white mushrooms, thinly sliced

4 bok choy, halved

½ cup bean sprouts

juice of 1 lime

a splash of fish sauce (if you have any)

2 scallions, shredded

Sweet potato Cullen Skink

It's that famous haddock and potato soup named after the Scottish fishing village called Cullen. As far as I'm aware, skink traditionally means meat soup—except, of course, in this case. Traditionally, Finnan haddie—smoked haddock from the fishing village of Findon, near Aberdeen—is used, but good-quality, undyed smoked haddock will do just fine. My untraditional version uses sweet potato, which matches the salty fish flavor very well indeed.

For a real treat, poach an egg and drop one into each bowl before serving.

1 Melt the butter in a large pan and cook the onion for 5 minutes, or until softened. Add the fish—you may need to cut it so it fits into the pan. Pour over the milk and bring to a boil. Reduce the heat, then cover the pan and simmer gently for 10 minutes.

2 Meanwhile, peel and cube, then cook the sweet potatoes in a pan of boiling water for 10–15 minutes, or until tender. Drain and mash coarsely.

3 Once the fish is cooked, lift it out of the pan and break into large flakes. Stir the mashed sweet potato into the pan along with the flaked fish and the parsley. Gently heat through, check the seasoning, then ladle into bowls (pop a poached egg into each first, if using) and serve.

Poaching eggs
Crack the eggs into a pan of just-simmering water and cook for 2 minutes. Take off the heat and let sit for 5 minutes, or until the whites are set, but the yolks are still a little soft.

Serves 4

a small knob of butter

1 small onion, peeled and finely chopped

1 lb 10 oz/800 g undyed smoked haddock fillets, skinned and boned

5 cups whole milk

2 sweet potatoes

2 tablespoons chopped fresh parsley

sea salt and freshly ground black pepper

4 poached eggs, to serve (optional)

Mega Fillers

Parsley Frittata

I've kept this very simple because I love the flavor of parsley. You can, however, dress it up by adding, for example, torn ham or diced cheese. It's great slipped out of the pan and eaten hot with a quick tomato salad, or cooled, then wrapped in foil and packed up for lunch (or breakfast) the next day.

1 Place the bread in a bowl, then cover with cold water and let stand for a few minutes.

2 Meanwhile, pop the garlic, chile, and parsley (leaves only) into a food processor and whiz until finely chopped. Drain the bread, then lightly squeeze out any excess water, but leaving it quite soggy. Add to the food processor and whiz again until well blended.

3 Crack the eggs into a large bowl and beat well together. Add the parsley and bread mixture, the Parmesan, and scallions, then season with salt and plenty of black pepper.

4 Heat the oil in an 8-inch/20-cm nonstick skillet. Pour the eggs into the hot pan and cook for 1 minute or so, stirring until the egg begins to set, then cook on the lowest heat for 6–7 minutes, or until the egg is almost completely set. Preheat the broiler to medium.

5 Place the pan under the preheated broiler for 2–3 minutes, or until the frittata is golden brown and cooked through. Slide onto a cutting board and cut into wedges. Serve with a tomato salad, prosciutto, and arugula.

Serves 4

1 thick slice of a day or two-day old rough white bread, about 2 oz/50 g

2 garlic cloves, peeled and coarsely chopped

1 red chile, seeded and coarsely chopped

1 large bunch of fresh parsley, preferably curly but flat-leaf is fine

6 eggs

2 tablespoons freshly grated Parmesan cheese

4 scallions, thinly sliced

1 tablespoon olive oil

sea salt and freshly ground black pepper

tomato salad, and maybe some sliced prosciutto and arugula, to serve

Myriam's milky macaroni with poached apples

My Swiss friend Myriam presents the cookery program on Swiss National Radio. She describes this as "the perfect dish for a rainy day," and says the poached apples help to digest "the fancy cheese and will save you the dessert." The apples are still delicious the day after. Myriam says "this dish is for four people; or one with a broken heart..."

1 For the poached apples, cut the apples in half and remove the core, then cut into fourths. Put the apples in a small pan, then add a squeeze of the lemon juice and cover with water. Bring to a boil, then reduce the heat and simmer for about 5 minutes, or until they are soft. Add some more lemon juice and the vanilla sugar to taste, and let stand for a while to cool.

2 Cook the macaroni in a pan of boiling water. In the meantime, melt the butter in a skillet, then add the onion and fry until soft and golden brown. Take off the heat, but keep the onions warm.

3 Heat the milk in a small pan and spice it with the bouillon powder, some freshly grated nutmeg, and black pepper.

4 Drain the hot macaroni and put half of it in a large serving dish. Evenly sprinkle half the grated cheese over it, then cover with the remaining macaroni and top with the rest of the cheese. Pour the milk mixture over and add more nutmeg, if desired. Spread the fried onions over it, then cover with a lid or some foil and let it rest for just 4–5 minutes to enable the cheese to melt.

5 To serve, place the macaroni on the table and pass the poached apples.

Serves 4

14 oz/400 g macaroni

1 teaspoon butter

1 large white onion, peeled

generous ¾ cup whole milk

a large pinch of vegetable bouillon powder

freshly grated nutmeg

7 oz/200 g Gruyère cheese, grated

freshly ground black pepper

For the poached apples

2 apples

juice of ½ lemon

½ teaspoon vanilla sugar (optional)

Thai spiced pork and rice noodles

This is an absolute classic, but one I'll never grow bored of. Traditionally the pork is served piled onto or rolled into lettuce leaves, but I've chosen instead to toss my leaves in with the mixture.

1 Place the noodles in a large heatproof bowl and pour over a kettleful of boiling water.

2 Heat the oil in a wok until smoking, then stir-fry the pork and garlic for 5 minutes, or until golden and cooked through. Tip into a large serving bowl.

3 Mix the fish sauce with the lime juice and chili sauce and stir into the hot pork with the onion, bean sprouts, and chopped chiles. Drain the noodles, then stir into the bowl and let settle for 5–10 minutes.

4 Stir in the lettuce and herbs and serve warm.

Serves 4

100 g/3½ oz vermicelli rice noodles

1 tablespoon peanut or sunflower-seed oil

1½ lb/750 g lean ground pork

2 garlic cloves, peeled and crushed

2 tablespoons fish sauce

juice of 2 limes

2 tablespoons sweet chili sauce

1 red onion, peeled and thinly sliced

⅔ cup bean sprouts

2 hot red chiles, finely chopped, seeds and all

2 Boston lettuce, leaves separated and torn

a large handful of fresh mint leaves

a large handful of fresh basil leaves

Shrimp udon noodles

I love udon noodles. They're made from wheat and are usually very thick and quite rounded strands—good for slurping! They can be bought dried from specialist stores, but are available in most supermarkets cooked and vacuum-packed in "straight-to-wok" packages. Make sure you use the Oriental chili oil with shrimp paste in it.

1 Place the noodles in a large heatproof bowl and cover with a kettleful of boiling water—they are meant to be "straight to wok," but boiling water loosens the noodles and stops them sticking to each other or breaking. Let stand for 5 minutes, then drain well.

2 Heat the oil in a large wok. Once it starts to smoke, add the noodles and shrimp and stir-fry over the highest heat for 4–5 minutes, or until the shrimp are pink and curled.

3 Keeping the heat at highest, stir in the chiles, scallions, bean sprouts, soy sauce, vinegar, and chili oil. Cook for a couple of minutes until piping hot, then turn out onto plates. Scatter over the peanuts and cilantro leaves and eat.

Serves 4

10 oz/300 g "straight-to-wok" (precooked) udon noodles

1 tablespoon sunflower-seed oil

1 lb 2 oz/500 g raw shelled jumbo shrimp, deveined

2 red chiles, thinly sliced, seeds and all

4 scallions, sliced

⅔ cup bean sprouts

1 tablespoon soy sauce

1 teaspoon rice or wine vinegar

1 teaspoon chili oil

⅓ cup salted peanuts, finely chopped

a handful of fresh cilantro leaves

Holiday squid and potatoes

I love squid! It reminds me, firstly, of my mum's kitchen, where she always dusts the rings in flour, then dips them in egg and fries them in olive oil, and, secondly, of being on holiday. We don't get served squid often enough in northern Europe, but in Italy, Portugal, and Spain every sidewalk restaurant and café has it on the menu. Serve with plain boiled potatoes and use the back of your fork to mash them into the lovely juices. The perfect lunch and good for you, too.

1 Place the garlic, tomatoes, basil, and oil in a small pan and cook for 10 minutes, or until the tomatoes are pulpy. Pour in the wine and bubble rapidly for 5 minutes, then stir in a splash of water.

2 Add the squid and cook for just a couple of minutes until it turns white and loses its translucency. Stir in the capers and parsley and add the lemon juice and seasoning to taste. Serve straightaway with boiled potatoes (or crusty bread).

Best boiled potatoes

Choose small white-skinned potatoes and put them whole into a pan of cold water. Bring to a boil, then reduce the heat and simmer until tender. Drain and, when just cool enough to handle, peel off the skins. Toss with a tiny splash of olive oil and a little sea salt.

Serves 2

4 garlic cloves, peeled and finely chopped

4 ripe tomatoes, finely chopped

a handful of fresh basil leaves

2 tablespoons olive oil

scant ½ cup red wine

14 oz/400 g cleaned squid, cut into rings

1 tablespoon capers, rinsed

4 tablespoons coarsely chopped fresh parsley

juice of ½ lemon

sea salt and freshly ground black pepper

boiled whole potatoes, to serve

Saffron-baked rice and chicken

This is sort of a cross between a risotto and a biriyani. It's a one-pot dish (which are always my favorites—life's too short for more than 5 minutes at the sink) and uses warm Med flavors and basmati rice with its elegant, separate grains. Pop it in the oven and forget all about it for about a half-hour.

1 Preheat the oven to 400°F/200°C. Stir the saffron into the hot stock and set aside.

2 Heat the oil in a large casserole or roasting pan and cook the chicken, onion, and garlic for 5 minutes or so until the onion has softened a little. Add the paprika and rosemary and cook for a couple of minutes more.

3 Stir in the tomatoes, rice, vinegar, and warm stock. Cover and pop in the oven for 20–30 minutes, or until the rice is tender and all the stock has been absorbed. Stir through the parsley and dish up.

Serves 4

a large pinch of saffron

3 cups hot chicken stock

1 tablespoon olive oil

8 cubed skinless boneless chicken thighs or 4 cubed skinless boneless breasts

1 red onion, peeled and thinly sliced

2 garlic cloves, peeled and thinly sliced

2 teaspoons smoked paprika

1 rosemary stem, broken into sprigs

4 tomatoes, coarsely chopped

2 cups basmati rice

1 teaspoon balsamic vinegar

1 bunch of fresh flat-leaf parsley, coarsely chopped

Pot-roast chicken with lemon and potatoes

Most of the recipes in this book are quick to cook; this one takes a little longer, but doesn't ask for much time in terms of preparation. Just pop it in the oven and come back to it later. Ask the butcher to chop up the bird for you if you're not sure about doing it yourself. The sour cream is not essential, but is very nice.

1 Preheat the oven to 400°F/200°C. Place the chicken pieces, lemon, onion, garlic, potatoes, and tarragon in a large ovenproof dish. Add some salt and pepper, then pour over the hot stock—it should come about halfway up the dish and some of the chicken and potatoes should be sitting out of the liquid.

2 Roast in the oven for 45 minutes, or until the chicken is cooked through and golden on the surface. Lift out and discard the lemon. Stir in the sour cream and serve.

Serves 4

1 large chicken, cut into 8 pieces

1 small thin-skinned unwaxed lemon, pierced once or twice with a knife

1 onion, peeled and finely chopped

4 garlic cloves, peeled and halved

4 red-skinned potatoes, peeled and cubed

a small handful of fresh tarragon leaves

generous 2 cups hot chicken stock

2 tablespoons sour cream

sea salt and freshly ground black pepper

Pork and charmoula burgers

Charmoula is a Moroccan spiced sauce or marinade and it does a brilliant job of livening up pork, which can be a bit on the bland side.

1 Using either a heavy knife or a pestle and mortar, crush the garlic with some salt to make a smooth paste. Stir in the paprika, cayenne, cumin, and vinegar to make the charmoula.

2 Mix the pork with the charmoula and cilantro and shape into 8 patties. Cook in a nonstick skillet for 5–6 minutes on each side, or until nicely browned and cooked through. Serve hot with the lemon wedges, some salad and chutney, or nice rice (see below).

Nice rice
There's a wonderful Lebanese takeaway on my local main street, where the hot skewers of spiced lamb always come with lots of nice extras such as pickled green chiles, crispy white cabbage salad, yogurty dips, and, best of all, their reddish short-grained rice. I'm not sure how they make it, but it is a delicious accompaniment to all grilled meats. For my version, I cook basmati rice in boiling water with a finely chopped tomato, a tiny pinch of saffron, and a small knob of butter.

Serves 4

2 garlic cloves, peeled

1 teaspoon paprika

1 teaspoon cayenne

1 teaspoon ground cumin

1 tablespoon red wine vinegar

1 lb 2 oz/500 g lean ground pork

2 tablespoons coarsely chopped fresh cilantro leaves

flaky sea salt

lemon wedges, for squeezing over

Spinach and goat cheese tart

Not much can beat a real homemade tart and this one takes no short cuts, although if you wish, do use ready-made unsweetened pastry. This is ideal for making the day before, but store in a cool, dry place rather than the refrigerator if you want to avoid a soggy bottom.

1 Preheat the oven to 400°F/200°C. Place both flours, the butter, and ½ teaspoon salt in a food processor and whiz until the mixture forms fine crumbs. Pour in the cold water and pulse again to form a firm dough.

2 Roll the pastry out on a floured counter and use to line a 9 inch/23 cm loose-bottom tart pan. Prick the base, then fill with crumpled foil and bake in the oven for 10 minutes. Remove the foil, then lower the oven to 350°F/180°C and return the shell to the oven for 3–4 minutes.

3 Wash the spinach well and cook in a pan or microwave until wilted, then squeeze out any excess water. Heat the butter in a skillet and cook the garlic for 2 minutes, or until softened but not colored. Stir in the spinach to coat it in the garlic butter, then remove from the heat.

4 Beat together the cream, milk, whole eggs and egg yolks, and chili flakes until well blended. Add a little salt and pepper.

5 Arrange the spinach and cheese in the tart shell and pour over the egg mixture. Bake in the oven for 25 minutes, or until golden and just set. Carefully remove the tart from the pan, then cut into slices and serve while still warm.

Serves 6
⅔ cup all-purpose flour, plus extra for dusting

scant ⅔ cup whole-wheat flour

⅞ stick chilled butter, diced

3 tablespoons very cold water

For the filling
9 oz/250 g fresh spinach

a small knob of butter

1 garlic clove, peeled and thinly sliced

scant ⅔ cup sour cream

1¼ cups whole milk

2 large eggs plus 2 yolks

½ teaspoon dried chili flakes

7 oz/200 g firm rinded goat cheese, diced

sea salt and freshly ground black pepper

Barley and butternut risotto

This takes a while to cook, as the vegetables are roasted separately, but the flavor they develop is worth the extra effort. This is fantastic packed into lunch boxes and eaten as a cold salad the next day.

Serves 4

1 medium carrot, sliced

1 small butternut squash, peeled, seeded and cut into ¾ inch/1.5 cm chunks

4 tablespoons extra virgin olive oil

1 onion, peeled and chopped

2 garlic cloves, peeled and coarsely chopped

scant 1 cup pearl barley

generous ¾ cup dry white wine

3 cups hot chicken or vegetable stock

2 fresh thyme sprigs

sea salt

freshly grated Parmesan cheese, to serve

1 Preheat the oven to 400°F/200°C. Toss the carrot and butternut squash with 2 tablespoons of the oil and some salt on a cookie sheet and spread out in an even layer. Roast in the oven until golden and tender, about 25 minutes.

2 Meanwhile, heat the remaining oil in a large pan. Cook the onion and garlic for a couple of minutes, then add the barley and cook, stirring occasionally, until the vegetables soften a bit, about 5 minutes.

3 Pour in the wine and cook, stirring frequently, until the liquid is absorbed. Add the hot stock and thyme, then reduce the heat and simmer fairly gently for 30–35 minutes, or until the liquid is absorbed and the barley is tender but still slightly firm.

4 Stir in the roasted vegetables and divide between bowls. Scatter over the Parmesan and serve.

Curried kipper fish cakes

I see no reason to be snooty about boil-in-the-bag kippers, if you can find them. I always keep a bag in the freezer for emergencies and love the fact I can boil the kippers and my eggs in the same pan if I want a quick kedgeree for Sunday breakfast. Of course, if you have a good local fish dealer with gorgeous fresh kippers, you must use them. A chopped hard-cooked egg makes a lovely addition.

1 Cook the potatoes in a large pan of boiling water until tender. Drain and mash thoroughly.

2 Meanwhile, cook the kippers according to the package directions, or place in a bowl, then cover with a kettleful of boiling water and set aside for 10 minutes.

3 Stir the chives or scallions, the curry paste, and peas into the potatoes. Skin the kippers and break the flakes into the potato mixture, then gently fold together. With floured hands, shape the mixture into 6–8 cakes.

4 Brush a large nonstick skillet with oil and cook the fish cakes for 5 minutes on each side, or until crisp, golden, and piping hot. Serve with salad greens.

Serves 4–6

1½ lb/750 g mealy white potatoes

14 oz/400 g kipper fillets

1 bunch of fresh chives or 4 scallions, finely chopped

1 tablespoon curry paste

½ cup frozen peas, thawed

all-purpose flour, for dusting

1 tablespoon sunflower-seed oil

salad greens, to serve

Fiery basil and broccoli penne

This recipe uses my favorite "double basil" method. The basil goes in at the beginning with the bacon where the flavor cooks in wonderfully and then it's added again at the end for a fresh, vibrant flavor. Yum. Try, too, with cauliflower instead of the broccoli.

1 Cook the pasta in a large pan of boiling salted water for 5 minutes. Add the broccoli and continue to cook until the pasta is just cooked and the broccoli is just a little bit overcooked.

2 Heat the oil in a small skillet and cook the onion, bacon, chiles, garlic, and half the basil for 8 minutes or so until the onions are nicely golden and the pasta is ready.

3 Drain the pasta and broccoli (use a large strainer, as you will lose a lot of the broccoli through the big holes of a colander) and return to the pan. Stir in the bacon and onion mixture, the remaining fresh basil leaves, and plenty of freshly ground black pepper. Squeeze in the lemon juice and serve with the grated cheese.

Serves 4

1 lb 2 oz/500 g package penne or fusilli

1 small head of broccoli, cut into small florets

1–2 tablespoons olive oil

1 small onion, chopped

2 strips lean bacon, chopped

2 hot red chiles, thinly sliced

2 garlic cloves, peeled and thinly sliced

a large bunch of fresh basil leaves

juice of ½ lemon

sea salt and freshly ground black pepper

freshly grated Parmesan or romano cheese, to serve

Stir-fried mushrooms with ginger and greens

I'm quite fussy about how I take my mushrooms—those white mushrooms, in particular, taste of nothing at all and don't have a very nice texture either. Some good cremini mushrooms, however, cooked with ginger, chiles, and soy sauce are a different deal altogether. For your greens choose an Oriental leaf such as bok choy or choi sum, young leaf spinach, or baby Swiss chard.

Serve with plain rice or noodles and, if you like them, scatter over some toasted cashews.

1 Put your wok on to get very hot. Meanwhile, mix all the ingredients for the dressing in a bowl and put to one side.

2 Once the wok is very hot, add the peanut or sunflower-seed oil, then stir-fry the ginger, garlic, and chile for 20 seconds. Add the mushrooms, scallions, and greens and stir-fry for a few minutes, until the mushrooms have taken on some color and the greens have wilted.

3 Pour in the dressing, then take off the heat and stir in the basil or cilantro. Eat straightaway.

Serves 2

1 tablespoon peanut or sunflower-seed oil

1½-inch/3.5-cm piece of fresh gingerroot, peeled and shredded

1 garlic clove, peeled and thinly sliced

1 hot red chile, thinly sliced

9 oz/250 g largish cremini mushrooms, halved

6 scallions, thickly sliced

a bowl of greens (see above)

a few fresh Thai parsley or basil or cilantro leaves

For the dressing

2 tablespoons light soy sauce

a pinch of superfine sugar

a pinch of flaky sea salt

1 teaspoon rice or wine vinegar

1 teaspoon sesame oil

1 tablespoon cold water

Asparagus and lemon rice

Brown rice is far more satisfying than its polished white counterparts. It's chewy and nutty and also takes longer to digest, so you get a good, slow release of energy. I've served it here with classic risotto flavorings and the result is delicious.

1 Heat the oil in a pan and cook the onion and garlic for 5 minutes until softened. Stir in the rice and cook for a minute or two, then pour over the boiling water and simmer for 30 minutes, or until the grains are tender.

2 Add the asparagus, then cover and continue to cook for an additional 5–7 minutes, or until the rice and asparagus are tender and all the liquid has been absorbed.

3 Stir in the lemon rind and juice and the mascarpone and season to taste.

Serves 4

1 tablespoon olive oil

1 small onion, peeled and finely chopped

2 garlic cloves, peeled and finely chopped

1½ cups brown rice

4 cups boiling water

11 oz/300 g thick asparagus spears, halved

grated rind and juice of 1 unwaxed lemon

2–3 tablespoons mascarpone or other soft cheese

sea salt and freshly ground black pepper

Big Salads

Chickpea salad with flat bread

This is very simple, but the combination of flavors makes it really enjoyable to eat. It's even better, though slightly stronger tasting, the next day. I've dressed this with avocado oil of which I am a fan (vitamin E and lovely flavor), but use olive oil if you'd rather.

1   Tip the chickpeas into a large bowl and stir in the feta, onion, and cilantro leaves. In a small bowl, whisk together the cumin seeds, chili flakes, oil, and lime rind and juice. Season with salt and pepper, then pour over the chickpeas, mixing well together. Let settle for 10 minutes if you've got the time.

2   Toast the flat breads or tortillas until crisp and dark golden. Spoon on the salad and eat.

Serves 2

14 oz/400 g canned chickpeas, drained and rinsed

3½ oz/100 g feta cheese, crumbled

1 small red onion, peeled and finely chopped

a handful of fresh cilantro leaves

1 teaspoon toasted cumin seeds

a large pinch of crushed chili flakes

2 tablespoons avocado oil

juice and grated rind of 1 unwaxed lime

2 Lebanese flat breads or flour tortillas

sea salt and freshly ground black pepper

Egg and potato salad

Boiled eggs and potatoes are always going to make a lovely salad. This one also has capers, olives, and anchovies and is dressed with a gorgeous mustard vinaigrette.

1 Put two pans of water on to boil—one small and one large. Cook the potatoes in the large pan for 20 minutes, or until tender. Add the eggs to the other pan and cook for 8 minutes. Cool, then shell and cut into fourths.

2 Next, make the vinaigrette. Place the garlic and ½ teaspoon sea salt in a mini food processor and whiz to a paste. Whiz in the mustard and vinegars and then the oil until well blended. Check the seasoning, adding salt and pepper to taste.

3 Drain the potatoes and place in a large bowl. Stir in the vinaigrette and shallots and let cool for 10 minutes.

4 Mix in the olives, anchovies, capers, and parsley and divide between serving bowls or plates. Top with the eggs and serve while still warm.

Serves 4

2¼ lb/1 kg new potatoes, halved if large

4 large eggs

4 shallots, peeled and finely chopped

generous ½ cup stuffed green olives, sliced

2 oz/50 g canned anchovies in olive oil, drained and coarsely chopped

4 tablespoons small capers, rinsed

1 large bunch of fresh parsley, coarsely chopped

For the vinaigrette

2 garlic cloves, peeled

1 teaspoon English mustard powder

1 tablespoon balsamic vinegar

1 tablespoon sherry or wine vinegar

scant ½ cup extra virgin olive oil

sea salt and freshly ground black pepper

Soba, watermelon, and feta salad

Soba noodles are made with buckwheat and are traditionally served either hot in soups or cold in salads. They can be replaced in this gorgeous salad with rice noodles, if preferred.

1 Cook the noodles in a pan of lightly salted boiling water for 3–4 minutes, or until tender. Tip them into a colander and place under cold running water until they are completely cold. Then give the colander a good shake to get rid of any excess water.

2 Gently toss the cooled noodles with the watermelon, cilantro leaves, feta, scallions, and sesame seeds. Whisk together the lime juice, oils, and black pepper and drizzle over the salad. Serve chilled.

Serves 4

5 oz/150 g soba noodles

¼ watermelon, cut into cubes

1 bunch of fresh cilantro leaves

7 oz/200 g block feta cheese, coarsely diced

2 scallions, finely chopped

1 tablespoon toasted sesame seeds

juice of 1 plump lime

1 tablespoon olive oil

1 teaspoon sesame oil

sea salt and freshly ground black pepper

Vinegar-rubbed lamb salad with herb couscous

Rubbing vinegar into the lamb produces a lovely flavor and has a tenderizing effect. Lamb sirloin is an expensive cut, but it's also very lean, which is essential for a just-warm salad.

1 Place the lamb in a dish with 2 tablespoons of the vinegar, the sugar, a little salt, and the garlic. Using your hands, massage the flavors into the lamb, then set aside for 5–10 minutes.

2 Meanwhile, pour the hot stock over the couscous and set aside. Preheat the broiler.

3 Discard the garlic and cook the lamb under the broiler, turning from time to time for 12–20 minutes. Let the lamb rest for 5 minutes, then slice.

4 Fluff up the couscous with a fork, then stir in the lamb's resting juices, the remaining vinegar, the oil, herbs, tomato, and shallot. (I like to leave this all to cool down a little and serve just warm, but it can be served hotter.)

5 Stir the arugula and lamb into the couscous and serve with the yogurt or tzatziki.

Serves 2

11 oz/300 g lamb sirloin

3 tablespoons red wine vinegar

a pinch of sugar

2 garlic cloves, peeled and cut into fourths

¾ cup hot chicken stock

5 oz/150 g couscous

2 tablespoons olive oil

2 tablespoons chopped fresh mint leaves

2 tablespoons chopped fresh parsley

1 ripe tomato, finely chopped

1 shallot, peeled and finely chopped

2 oz/50 g wild arugula

sea salt

strained plain yogurt or tzatziki, to serve

Rosemary-roasted chicken and sweet potato salad

This is simple to make and fantastic served warm, or chilled and packed into a box for a perfect picnic or desktop lunch. If you feel like pushing this recipe a bit further, top with a few cubes of gentle blue cheese such as Dolcelatte or a mild Gorgonzola.

1 Preheat the oven to 425°F/220°C. Place the chicken pieces skin-side up in a large shallow roasting pan with the sweet potatoes and tomatoes. Tuck in the garlic and rosemary. Drizzle over 1 tablespoon of the oil, then sprinkle with salt and pepper and the fennel seeds if you have them. Roast in the oven for 20–25 minutes, or until the chicken is golden and cooked through and the sweet potatoes are tender.

2 Dress with the lime juice and remaining oil, then let cool in the pan for a good 10 minutes.

3 If eating warm, toss with the watercress and divide between bowls. If serving cold, dress the chicken with the oil and lime juice as before, but let cool completely before tossing with the watercress.

Serves 4

4 skin-on boneless chicken thighs, each cut into 6

2 large sweet potatoes, peeled and cut into chunks

3½ oz/100 g cherry tomatoes

4 whole unpeeled garlic cloves

4 rosemary stems, broken into sprigs

2 tablespoons olive oil

1 teaspoon fennel seeds (not essential but nice if you have them)

juice of 1 lime

1 bunch of watercress

sea salt and freshly ground black pepper

Anchovy panzanella

Panzanella is a classic Tuscan salad traditionally made with day-old bread. This version is made special by the addition of fresh oil-and-herb-marinated anchovy fillets—you can buy these in some supermarkets and from the counter in most delis.

1 Preheat the oven to 400°F/200°C. Scatter the bread cubes in a single layer onto a large nonstick cookie sheet. Bake in the oven for 12 minutes, or until crunchy and golden.

2 Arrange the tomatoes on a second cookie sheet and bake for 10 minutes, or until the skins split and the tomatoes begin to soften. Using a pair of scissors, snip the vines between each tomato to separate them.

3 To make the dressing, drain the oily marinade from the anchovies or seafood salad into a bowl. Add the tomato paste and vinegar, then use a fork to lightly whisk them together.

4 Arrange the bread, tomatoes, chile peppers, anchovy fillets or seafood salad, and the basil on a large serving platter. Drizzle over the dressing and serve.

Serves 4

1 large ciabatta loaf, cubed

1 lb/450 g cherry tomatoes on the vine

7 oz/200 g marinated fresh anchovy fillets or seafood salad in oil

1 tablespoon sun-dried tomato paste

1 tablespoon red wine vinegar

13 oz/375 g jar sweet pickled chile peppers, drained

1 bunch of fresh basil

Hot-smoked salmon with minted coleslaw

Hot-smoked salmon is now readily available and is great for salads and sandwiches. The soft oily salmon is really well complemented by the crisp and crunchy white cabbage.

1 Using either a heavy knife or a pestle and mortar, crush the garlic with some salt to make a smooth paste. Stir in the lime juice, oil, and caraway seeds to make a dressing.

2 Place the cabbage, onion, and mint in a large bowl and toss with the dressing. Divide between plates and top with the salmon, either whole or flaked.

Serves 4

1 small garlic clove, peeled

juice of 1 lime

3 tablespoons extra virgin olive oil

1 teaspoon caraway seeds

1 small white cabbage, about 9 oz/250 g, shredded

1 small red onion, peeled and thinly sliced

1 bunch of fresh mint leaves, coarsely torn

4 x 4–5 oz/125–150 g fillets hot-smoked salmon

flaky sea salt

Green lentil salad with arugula and crispy bacon

Green lentils make a lovely salad base and go particularly well with the crispy, salty bacon and peppery arugula. This recipe uses canned lentils for speed, but to cook your own, use 4oz (125g) dried green lentils and boil for 20 minutes until tender.

1 Place the bacon on a broiler rack and cook under a medium broiler for about 8 minutes, turning once, until crisp.

2 Meanwhile, heat the oil in a skillet and cook the onion, garlic, and rosemary for 5 minutes. Add the lentils and heat until just warmed through. Stir in the sour cream, mixing until it melts to coat the lentils, then stir in the vinegar and take off the heat. Check the seasoning, adding salt and pepper to taste.

3 Toss in the arugula or salad greens and divide between two bowls. Break the bacon into pieces and scatter on top. Serve just warm.

Serves 2

6 strips lean bacon

1 tablespoon olive oil

1 red onion, peeled and finely chopped

2 garlic cloves, peeled and finely chopped

2 tablespoons fresh rosemary leaves

14 oz/400 g canned cooked green lentils, drained

4 tablespoons half-fat sour cream

1 tablespoon balsamic vinegar

2½ oz/60 g arugula or baby salad greens

sea salt and freshly ground black pepper

Fig and ham plate

This is a simple antipasti-style salad and it makes a lovely, smart-looking lunch. The mixture of sweet, salty, and bitter flavors all together on one plate make this really exciting to eat.

Arrange the mango, figs, ham, endive, and cheese on two plates. Splash over a little oil and vinegar and serve with warmed crusty bread.

Serves 2

1 small ripe mango, peeled, pitted, and sliced

3 ripe figs, cut into fourths

4 slices of cured ham

1 head endive/chicory, separated into leaves

3 oz/75 g creamy blue cheese, such as Dolcelatte, Cambazola, Roquefort, or Gorgonzola, diced

extra virgin olive oil and balsamic vinegar, to serve

Peppered tuna and fava bean salad

I must be the only person on the planet who isn't mad for fresh tuna, but I'm afraid I much prefer it canned, especially when you can now get such lovely fillets in spring water or good olive oil. And I don't think you can really have too much pepper, it warms the back of your throat in such a pleasing way. And yes, it's good for you, too: black pepper improves digestion and has impressive antioxidant and antibacterial effects and, best of all, the outer layer stimulates the breakdown of fat cells! Not that I've noticed.

1 Cook the beans in a pan of boiling water for 4–5 minutes, or until tender. If you can face it, pop the beans out of their shells — personally, I think it's worth it; the shells are quite tough and the color of the beans within is so bright and pretty.

2 Next, empty the tuna fish into a strainer fitted over a bowl and let it drain, reserving the oil.

3 Using either a heavy knife or a pestle and mortar, crush the garlic with some salt to make a paste, then work the mustard powder into this. Push the mixture to one side, add the peppercorns and crush coarsely. Stir in the lemon rind and juice and 3 tablespoons of the reserved tuna oil (the rest can be discarded).

4 Arrange the arugula, tuna, onion, and beans on 4 plates and drizzle over the dressing. Serve with chunks of warm crusty bread.

Serves 4

2¾ cups frozen fava beans

14 oz/400 g canned tuna fillets in olive oil

2 garlic cloves, peeled

1 teaspoon English mustard powder

2 teaspoons black peppercorns

grated rind and juice of 1 unwaxed lemon

2 oz/50 g arugula

1 red onion, peeled and sliced into thin circles

flaky sea salt

Harissa'd chicken tabbouleh

Harissa is a Moroccan hot chili sauce that's really potent. There are lots of varieties around now, but choose the coarser ones rather then the super smooth pastes, as the texture is so much better. Look out too for different versions—my favorite is a rose harissa that's stocked in my local supermarket. Rub it into any chicken, meat, or fish before grilling or broiling.

1 Place the bulgur in a large bowl. Cover it with plenty of cold water and let stand for about 20 minutes, or until the grains soften.

2 Meanwhile, cook the chicken under a medium broiler for 8 minutes on each side, or until cooked through. Cut into slices.

3 In a large serving bowl, mix the harissa with the lemon juice and oil. Stir in the chicken and set aside for a few minutes, or until the bulgur is ready.

4 Line a colander with a clean tea towel and tip in the softened bulgur. Squeeze the cloth to get rid of as much excess water as possible. Stir into the serving bowl along with the scallions, tomatoes, herbs, cucumber, and chicken. Check the seasoning and serve.

Serves 4

11 oz/300 g bulgur wheat

2 large skinless boneless chicken breasts

1 tablespoon harissa paste

juice of 1 lemon

3 tablespoons olive oil

1 bunch of scallions, finely chopped

4 ripe tomatoes, chopped

1 large bunch of fresh mint, chopped

1 large bunch of fresh parsley, chopped

½ cucumber, coarsely chopped

sea salt and freshly ground black pepper

goat cheese and pomegranate couscous with pine nuts

Perfect lunchbox material. This salad keeps very well and has a great balance of flavors and textures. And pomegranates are very good for you—did you know, the ancient Egyptians were so keen on them that they included them in their tombs to ensure safe passage to the next world? Anyway, pomegranate is particularly good for the cardiovascular system and is useful for maintaining healthy blood pressure and cholesterol levels.

1 Place the couscous in a large bowl and cover with the hot stock. Set aside for 10 minutes, or until the grains are tender and all the liquid has been absorbed.

2 Mix the oil with the molasses and lime juice to make the dressing.

3 Using a fork, fluff up the couscous, then gently stir through the cheese, pomegranate seeds, herbs, and pine nuts. Stir in the dressing and chill until ready to serve.

Serves 2

5 oz/150 g couscous

¾ cup hot chicken or vegetable stock

2 tablespoons extra virgin olive oil

1 tablespoon pomegranate molasses

juice of ½ lime

2 x 3½ oz/100 g slices of firm goat cheese, crumbled

seeds of 1 pomegranate

2 tablespoons chopped fresh cilantro or mint leaves

2 tablespoons toasted pine nuts

Pasta and crab salad

I love the combination of pasta and crab. Canned crab is an excellent pantry ingredient and as well as being very low in fat, it is high in zinc, which is good for, among other things, healthy sensory function, meaning it'll help you to enjoy the smell and taste of your food even more. This is lovely served hot, but is a little nicer as a room-temperature salad.

1 Cook the pasta in a pan of boiling salted water according to the package directions. Drain the pasta into a colander.

2 Mix the crab, lemons, oil, garlic, chile, lemon juice, cilantro leaves, a little salt, and plenty of black pepper together in the hot pan. Add the drained pasta, tossing well so it is well coated in oil, herbs and crab.

3 Let sit for 5 minutes—it will stick together a little bit; how much depends on the type of pasta and shape you used. Eat when you're ready.

Serves 2

8 oz/225 g pasta shapes

6 oz/170 g canned white crab meat, drained

2 small preserved lemons, finely chopped

3 tablespoons olive oil

1 garlic clove, peeled and crushed

1 red chile, finely chopped

1 tablespoon fresh lemon juice

2 tablespoons chopped fresh cilantro leaves

sea salt and freshly ground black pepper

Roasted provolone and eggplant salad

I love pink peppercorns and just can't understand why they're so unfashionable. Their sweet flavor is lovely and delicate and goes very nicely with the orange I've used in the dressing. If, like everyone, you can't bear to use them either, ordinary old black peppercorns will do.

1 Preheat the oven to 400°F/200°C. Toss together the eggplant, tomatoes, cheese, and oil. Place on a shallow sheet in a single layer so they roast rather than steam. Roast in the oven for 25–30 minutes, or until the eggplant is cooked through and nicely browned.

2 Meanwhile, to make the dressing, mix the orange rind and juice with the oil, herbs, peppercorns, and some salt.

3 Tip the cooked eggplant, tomatoes, and cheese into a large bowl and stir in the dressing. Let sit for 5 minutes.

4 Divide the baby greens between 2 bowls and spoon the dressed warm salad on top.

Serves 2

1 large eggplant, cut into small cubes

9 oz/250 g cherry tomatoes

9 oz/250 g block of provolone cheese, cut into small cubes

2 tablespoons olive oil

2 oz/50 g baby salad greens

For the dressing

grated rind and juice of 1 small unwaxed orange

1 tablespoon extra virgin olive oil

1 tablespoon chopped fresh dill or tarragon leaves

1 teaspoon dried pink peppercorns, lightly crushed

sea salt

Seared beef salad with beet and green beans

You need a lovely piece of trimmed organic fillet of beef for this fantastic salad. It cooks best if you take it out of the refrigerator a good 30 minutes beforehand.

1 Cook the beans in a pan of boiling water for 4 minutes, then drain and cool.

2 Rub the beef with the oil, then roll it in the sesame seeds to coat. Cook in a hot pan for 7 minutes, turning from time to time until nicely browned. Let rest for 5 minutes.

3 Very thinly slice the beet—this is most easily done using a mandolin or other slicing machine. Separate the slices onto a platter. In a small bowl, mix the lime juice with the fish sauce, sugar, and chile. Once the sugar has dissolved, stir in the shallot, then pour the mixture over the beet. Set aside for 5–10 minutes.

4 Thinly slice the beef and toss with the beet, mint, lettuce leaves, and green beans.

Serves 4

9 oz/250 g green beans

14 oz/400 g fillet of beef

1 teaspoon vegetable oil

2 teaspoons sesame seeds

2 small fresh beets

juice of 1 lime

2 tablespoons fish sauce

1 teaspoon superfine sugar

1 small hot chile, thinly sliced

1 shallot, peeled and thinly sliced

2 tablespoons chopped fresh mint leaves

2 Boston lettuce, leaves separated

Final Finish

Good shortbread

Okay, so if we're being healthy, we shouldn't really be eating cookies, but we're all allowed a little bit of what we fancy once in a while and homemade is the way to go —at least you can be sure your cookies are additive free!

Makes 35

¾ stick salted butter, at room temperature

scant ¼ cup superfine sugar

scant ¼ cup semolina

½ cup all-purpose flour

1 Preheat the oven to 350°F/180°C. Using electric beaters, whisk the butter and sugar together for 5 minutes, or until pale. With a wooden spoon, beat in the semolina and flour.

2 Roll the mixture into cherry-size balls and place on a couple of nonstick cookie sheets. Bake in the oven for 20 minutes, or until golden, then let cool.

Oat-crunch summer fruit crumble

Make this all year round using a package of colorful, vitamin-rich, frozen summer fruits. Adding oats to a crumble is nothing new, but it just works so well! Nice warm from the oven, better cold the next day.

Serves 6

1 lb 2 oz/500 g bag frozen summer fruits, thawed

4 tablespoons blackcurrant or elderflower cordial

½ cup all-purpose flour

scant ½ cup whole-wheat flour

1 teaspoon ground allspice

¾ stick cold butter, diced

⅔ cup oatmeal

generous ⅓ cup demerara sugar

1 Preheat the oven to 375°F/190°C. Empty the fruits into a large shallow baking dish, then stir in the cordial.

2 Mix the flours with the allspice, then rub in the butter until there are no large pieces left. Stir in the oats and sugar.

3 Scatter the crumble over the fruit and bake in the oven for 40–45 minutes, or until nicely browned. Eat warm or cold.

Blueberry and banana puddings

People with a sweet tooth tend to enjoy proper old-fashioned steamed puddings. The problem is they are high in calories, low in nutrients, and take so long to cook. This lighter version includes fresh fruit and also has a cheats' method, where individual puds can be micro-cooked in just 3 minutes!

1 Place the butter, sugar, flours, baking powder, salt, and lemon rind in a large mixing bowl, then break in the eggs and whisk together, preferably with an electric hand-held whisk, until you have a soft creamy mixture.

2 Mash the bananas and stir into the mixture with the blueberries. Spoon the mixture into a 4-cup buttered pudding basin and level off the surface.

3 Take a square of double thickness foil and smear it with a little butter. Make a pleat in the center and fix it over the pudding, tying securely around the rim with string. Place the pudding in a pan, then pour in boiling water to come halfway up the side of the basin. Cover and steam for 2½ hours. Check halfway through cooking that the water in the pan isn't getting too low and top up with boiling water, if necessary.

4 Turn out and serve hot with custard.

Super-speedy version
Divide the mixture between 6 microwave-proof molds such as teacups. Microwave on High for 2½–3 minutes, or until risen and firm. Let stand for 1 minute before serving.

Serves 8

⅞ stick butter, softened, plus a little extra for greasing

½ cup light muscovado sugar

⅔ cup self-rising flour

scant ⅓ cup whole-wheat flour

½ teaspoon baking powder

a pinch of salt

grated rind of 1 unwaxed lemon

2 large eggs

2 ripe bananas

½ cup dried blueberries

Papaya and lime granita

Papaya is a wonder-fruit. It's low in calories but high in nutrients. It is an excellent source of beta-carotene, folate, and fiber and just one half contains 150% of the recommended daily amount of vitamin C. It is also said to have healing properties, and when rubbed onto a cut will speed up the healing. And it tastes very good, too, especially when paired with lime.

1 Place the sugar, lime rind and juice, lemongrass stalk, and ⅔ cup of the water in a pan. Heat gently, stirring until the sugar dissolves, then simmer gently for 5 minutes. Turn off the heat and let cool.

2 Meanwhile, halve the fruit, then scoop out the seeds and discard. Then scoop out the flesh and whiz in a food processor until smooth.

3 Strain the lime syrup into a rigid container, then stir in the remaining water and the papaya purée. Freeze for 2 hours until almost firm, then, using a fork, break the mixture into large flaky crystals. Freeze for an additional 2 hours, then break up again.

Serves 6

generous ½ cup superfine sugar

grated rind and juice of 4 unwaxed limes

1 lemongrass stalk, coarsely flattened with a rolling pin

2½ cups water

2 ripe papaya

Raspberry and rose-water whips

This is incredibly simple to make but looks gorgeous. Raspberries and roses are a fantastic union.

Serves 4

1⅔ cups fresh raspberries

¼ cup superfine sugar

a few drops of rose water

9 oz/250 g mascarpone

9 oz/250 g strained plain yogurt

pink rose petals, to decorate (optional)

1 Mash the raspberries, sugar, and rose water together to a pulp.

2 In a separate bowl, whisk together the mascarpone and yogurt, then ripple through the raspberries. Spoon into small serving glasses and chill until ready to eat. Decorate with rose petals, if you like.

Vanilla and cardamom-scented plums in port

This recipe is courtesy of my good friend and fellow food writer Jenny White. It does contain alcohol, but only one glassful for four servings and it has no added fat!

Serves 4

⅔ cup ruby port

⅔ cup water

2 tablespoons superfine sugar

2 strips lemon rind

1 vanilla bean, split lengthwise

1 cardamom pod, bruised

8 ripe, firm plums, halved and pitted

strained plain yogurt, to serve

1 Put the port in a pan with the water, sugar, lemon rind, vanilla bean, and cardamom pod. Heat gently, stirring until the sugar has dissolved, then add the plums and increase the heat. Simmer for 10–15 minutes, or until the plums are tender but retain their shape.

2 With a slotted spoon, divide the plums between 4 serving dishes. Continue boiling the port mixture until syrupy and reduced by half. Strain the syrup and spoon over the plums. Serve warm or chilled with yogurt.

Grape Jellies

Couldn't be easier! There are some really good-quality grape juices available now—they come in a variety of pretty colors and are naturally sweet, so all you need to do is set them.

1 Place the gelatin in a shallow dish of cold water and let stand for 5 minutes, or until softened.

2 Heat ⅔ cup of the grape juice in a small pan until hot but not boiling. Drain the gelatin leaves and squeeze out the excess water. Add to the pan, then turn off the heat and stir until dissolved. Let cool.

3 Add the rest of the grape juice to the gelatin mixture, then pour into 6 glasses (or plastic pots if you're planning a picnic). Scatter the blueberries on top if you have them, then cover and chill for at least a couple of hours until set.

Serves 6
5 sheets of leaf gelatin
2½ cups red grape juice
⅔ cup fresh blueberries (if you have any)

Buttermilk baked custard with orange strawberries

Buttermilk is lower in fat than regular milk since the fat has been used to make butter. It is also rich in vitamins and calcium and those who find milk difficult to digest may find buttermilk preferable, as it digests more quickly. It has a gentle sour tang to it, which makes it a good substitute for yogurt and sour cream.

1 Preheat the oven to 325°F/170°C. In a large pitcher, gently whisk together the whole eggs, egg yolks, buttermilk, sugar, cornstarch, and vanilla extract, but not too vigorously because you don't want to make bubbles.

2 Set a deep 8–9 inch/20–23 cm round ovenproof dish on a cookie sheet. Pour in the milk mixture and grate over some nutmeg. Bake in the oven for 30 minutes, or until the filling is golden brown, just about firm in the center, and slightly puffed up. Be careful not to overcook, as custard can develop a clotted texture that is not as nice as when it's smooth, although it will still taste good.

3 Meanwhile, place the strawberries, orange rind and juice, and sugar in a shallow heatproof dish and roast alongside the custard for 15 minutes. Serve warm or chilled.

Serves 4
3 large eggs plus 2 large egg yolks

scant 2½ cups buttermilk

¼ cup superfine sugar

1 teaspoon cornstarch

½ teaspoon vanilla extract

freshly grated nutmeg

For the strawberries
1 lb/450 g strawberries

juice and grated rind of 1 unwaxed orange

1 teaspoon superfine sugar

Coffee and walnut cake

A coffee cake in such a wholesome book? Well, yes. Firstly, coffee does have its merits: a study has found it contributes more antioxidants (which have been linked with fighting heart disease and cancer) to the diet than cranberries, apples, or tomatoes. And secondly, who can really be expected to live without cake once in a while?

1 Preheat the oven to 350°F/180°C. Dissolve the coffee in the 2 tablespoons of boiling water, then set aside to cool for a while. Take out the 12 prettiest walnut halves and chop the rest.

2 Place the flour, baking powder, butter, sugar, and eggs in a large bowl and whisk with electric beaters until well blended. Whisk in the cooled coffee, then stir in the chopped walnuts. Spoon the mixture into two lined nonstick 8-inch/20-cm cake pans. Bake in the oven for 30 minutes, or until the cakes feel a bit springy when touched.

3 Meanwhile, combine in a bowl all the ingredients for the filling.

4 For the syrup, dissolve the coffee and sugar in a boiling water. Remove the cakes from the oven. Pierce the cakes with a skewer, then drizzle over the syrup and let cool.

5 Once cooled, sandwich the cake together with half the filling. Smooth the rest of the filling on top of the cake and decorate with the reserved walnut halves—make sure there's one on each slice. Put the kettle on!

Serves 12

4 teaspoons instant espresso coffee powder

2 tablespoons boiling water

scant 1 cup walnut halves

scant 1¼ cups self-rising flour

1 teaspoon baking powder

1½ sticks butter, at room temperature

generous ¾ cup superfine sugar

3 large eggs, at room temperature

For the filling

1 tablespoon instant espresso coffee powder

2 tablespoons superfine sugar

1⅛ cups Quark or other lowfat soft cheese

⅞ cup mascarpone

For the syrup

1 tablespoon instant espresso coffee powder

¼ cup superfine sugar

5 tablespoons boiling water

Iced apple mint tea

This is a fantastic summer drink. Use good-quality pressed apple juice or, for the best result, juice some Granny Smiths yourself.

Serves 2
12 fresh mint leaves
1 tea bag
1¾ cups boiling water
generous ¾ cup pressed fresh apple juice
1 green apple, sliced
ice and mint leaves, to serve

1 Place the mint and tea bag in a pitcher and pour over a boiling water. Let cool, then strain into a pitcher. Stir in the apple juice and chill until ready to serve.

2 Stack the sliced apple, ice, and mint into 2 tall glasses and pour in the tea. Slip in straws and slurp.

Lemon barley water

Lemon drinks are very cleansing. While it's hard to knock good old-fashioned homemade lemonade, this barley water definitely has the edge over it. Try it with oranges, too.

Serves 2
generous ¼ cup pearl barley
4 cups boiling water
1 small unwaxed lemon
2½ cups cold water
1 tablespoon superfine sugar

1 Place the barley in a strainer and pour over the boiling water to scald and cleanse it (this aids in producing a clearer color for the finished barley water).

2 Finely peel the lemon, trying to avoid the pith, then squeeze the juice. Place the barley, lemon rind, and the cold water into a pan, then cover and simmer gently for 20 minutes.

3 Strain the liquid through a cheesecloth into a pitcher, then stir in the lemon juice and sugar to taste. Let cool, then chill, or serve over ice.

Real ginger beer

I always find making ginger beer exciting—the fizz that builds up is amazing, which is why you must use plastic bottles since glass can explode. Ginger beer is simple to make and doesn't take much effort but you do need to plan ahead—I promise it really will be the highlight of your picnic, so it's worth the trouble. I choose active dry yeast, not quick-rising or bread-machine yeast. Remember that because of the fermentation process this does develop a slight alcohol content.

Serves 8

2 tablespoons finely chopped fresh gingerroot

1 unwaxed lemon, thinly sliced

1¼ cups superfine sugar

9 cups cold water

½ teaspoon cream of tartar

½ x ¼ oz/7 g envelope active dry yeast

3 x 1 quart/1 liter plastic bottles (or 2 x 1½ quarts/ 1.5 liters)

1 Place the ginger, lemon, sugar, and generous 2 cups of the water in a large pan. Bring to a boil and simmer for 5 minutes. Pour in the remaining 7 cups of water and stir in the cream of tartar and the yeast. Cover and let stand overnight at room temperature.

2 Strain the liquid through a nylon strainer, then pour into clean plastic bottles, leaving a 2 inch/5 cm gap at the top. Screw on the caps and store in a cool place. Check the bottles once or twice a day—if they begin to expand outward, unscrew the cap to let some of the gas escape.

3 The ginger beer should be fizzy enough in about 12 hours, but will last up to 3 days, if kept chilled—remember to keep an eye on the fizz build-up. It should taste wonderfully of ginger and lemon, so don't drink it if it's at all musty or yeasty.

Index